Baby Names
for
GIRLS

Vijaya Kumar

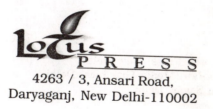

Lotus PRESS

4263 / 3, Ansari Road,
Daryaganj, New Delhi-110002

929.4095

Lotus Press
4263/3, Ansari Road, Darya Ganj, New Delhi-110002
Ph.: 32903912, 23290047
E-mail : lotus_press@sify.com

Baby Names for Girls
© 2007 Lotus Press
ISBN 81-8382-123-5

Published by: Lotus Press, New Delhi.
Lasertypeset by: Jain Media Graphics, Delhi.
Printed at: Gyan Sagar, Delhi

Choosing Your Baby's Name

Your baby is coming — very great news for you as parents as well as for your parents and everybody in the family — families of both the partners. It may as well be that grand-parents are much more excited than you are, and have already busied themselves with selecting the right name for the soon, arriving little guest, along with other related chores.

So, don't worry any of you because here is a book that provides thousands of names collected from various sources — traditional, new entrants and western as well as now quite favoured Christian and Muslim sources - the world is being truly globalised. And it is okay if your child has a more modern name, because a decade or so hence, when he will grow up, life on the planet will present a totally different shape. And if you prefer traditional names, you are free to do so.

Go ahead and have your choice.

Pronunciation
ā   as in *a*rm
ū   as in t*oo*
th as in *th*ermal
ṭh as in pa*th* (lesson)
ñ   as in gu*nn* (virtue)
ḍ   as in *d*id
ṭ   as in *t*ea

A

Ānandamayi: very happy.

Āpt: trustworthy, friend.

Āpti: fulfilment.

Āradhana: worship.

Ārushi: daughter of Manu.

Ārzoo: wish.

Āshalata: creeper of hope.

Āshrita: one who has taken refuge in the Lord.

Āshita: one who is hopeful.

Ababa: flower.

Abayomi: she who brings joy.

Abdhija: born in sea, Goddess Lakshmi.

Ābhā: splendour, beauty, likeness

Abharan: a jewel, ornament.

Abhayankari: one who gives courage, dispels fear.

Abharika: one who has a halo around her head, a Goddess.

Abhaya: fearlessness, courage.

Abhidhā: name

Abhigeetha: praised.

Abhijaata (Abhijata): Well born woman.

Abhijaya: victorious.

Abhijishya: independent girl.

Abhijita (Abhijitha): victorious woman.

Abhikhya: beauty, fame, shine.

Abhilashita: desired, yearned for.

Abhimanini: who possesses self-respect.

Abhigyā: intelligent, ingenious

Abhilāshā: desire, wish

Abhinandana: congratulations, happiness.

Abhinetri : actress, dancer.

Abhinivesha: long cherished desire, faith, Determination.

Abhiroopa: beautiful woman, attractive.

Abhiraksha: protector

1

Abhirami: beautiful

Abhisarika: beloved

Abhishikta: laughing girl.

Abhivandya: one who is respected, saluted

Abhitā: fearless

Abhivibhā: illuminant

Abigail (Abigal): rejoices, delightful, name of king David's third wife

Abimola: born to the rich

Abiona: born while journeying

Abira: strong

Abirami: Lakshmi.

Abjini: lotus pond, collection of lotuses.

Abline: white

Acacia: thorny

Acantha: from the plant Acanthus

Acchoda: limpid water, pure water, name of a pond in heaven.

Acelin: dream

Achalā: earth, immovable

Acheerā: swift, prompt, brief, active

Achinā: carefree

Achintya: beyond thought

Achira: very short

Achiraprabha: lightening

Acie: thorny

Ada: joyous, prosperous.

Adabelle: joyous and fair

Adag: pure, blemishless

Adalia: refuge of God, just, noble

Adama: feminine of Adam

Adanna: father's daughter

Adarā: beauty

Adarsha (Aadarsha): ideal, aim

Adbhutha: marvel, astounding

Addis: new

Adelaide: noble, kindly, cheerful

Adela: noble

Adeline: of noble birth

Aderet: cape

Adharshana: idealistic

Adhidevata: patron diety, presiding diety

Adhika: excess, abundant, special

Adhrishyā: invisible

2

Adhrushta: goodluck, fortune

Adhya: beyond imagination

Adija: of the mountain, an apsara's name

Adil: sincere

Adina: graceful, delicate

Adisri (Aadisree): Adi Lakshmi

Adishyanti: invincible, sage Parashar's mother

Adita: the first root

Aditi: perfection, freedom, safety, abundance

Adiva: pleasant, gentle

Adna: pleasure

Adney: pleasure

Adrija: Parvati

Adrika: small hill

Aduke: beloved

Adya: first, excellent, earth, Durga

Afra: young doe, earth colour, from the continent Africa

Afreen: encouragement

Aftab: the Sun

Aftan: from Afton

Aganit: countless, innumerable, infinite, god, Vishnu.

Aganjita: the conqueror of fire

Agasthi: a learned lady of the past

Agasthya: a star

Agatha: good, pure, kind

Aghamarshan: destroyer of sin

Aghanashini: destroyer of sins, river

Agneji: daughter of fire, Kuru's wife, daughter of Agni

Agnes: pure, chaste, true

Agnidevi: the fire goddess

Agnije: Agni's daughter, Draupadi

Agnimitra: Agni's friend, the wind

Agninayan: Shiva.

Agraja: born first, elder daughter

Agrasandhya: sunrise, dawn.

Agrata (Agratha): leadership.

Agrima: leadership

Ahalyā: agreeable, sage Gautama's wife

Ahanā: one who cannot be killed, immortal, day-born

Ahanti: Name of west African tribe.

Ahava: beloved.

Ahi: heaven and earth conjoined

Ahava: beloved

Ahladini: joyous person, lady in happy mood, happy lady

Ahladitā: delighted

Ahladitha: joyous person. Lady in happy mood. Happy lady

Ahobal: mighty, Hanuman

Āhuti: summoning, offering

Ahwānā: call, summon

Ahwaintha: who has invented, wanted

Aiḍa: joyful, helper, reward

Aiesha: woman

Aileen: light, green meadow

Aikshvāki: very sweet

Aimee: beloved friend

Aina: eternal.

Aisha: life, woman, the favourite wife of Mohammed

Aisheeya: ocean.

Aishwaryā: wealth, glory, fame

Aislinn: vision, daydream

Aissa: grateful

Aiyana: everlasting bloom, forever flowering.

Aizlyn: dream.

Aja: she goat, Shakti

Ajaamil: unfriendly

Ajabu: rare

Ajaganda: daughter of Aja.

Ajala: the Earth

Ajamukhi: daughter of sage Kashyap and Surase.

Ajātā: eternal, another name for earth

Ajath: birthless, Shiva, Vishnu, Jina.

Ājāni: of noble birth

Ajarā: ever youthful, river Saraswati

Ajathyā: yellow jasmine

4

Ajayā: unconquerable

Ajeeba: wonder

Ajeerā: quick, agile, Durga

Ajeya : one who cannot be conquered, Vishnu.

Ajinkya: one who cannot be conquered.

Ajitā: unconquerable

Ajitesha: Vishnu.

Akalanka: faultless, flawless

Ākaliki: lightning

Akalmasha: pure.

Ākānkshā: desire, wish

Ākāshdeepā: a lamp in the sky, bright

Ākāshgangā: the Milky Way, the celestial Ganga

Ākāshi: all-pervading, atmosphere

Akhilā: intelligent

Akhileswari: Lalithamba's other name.

Akhira: white Lilly.

Akifā: devoted, dedicated

Akihlandeshwari: queen of the world, Parvati.

Akrant: might, force.

Ākrānti: valour, force

Ākriti: form, shape

Akshamālā: a rosary of Rudraksha seeds

Akshata:unscated, perfect.

Akshayā: undecaying, the goddess of earth

Akshayamathi: super intelligence, divyagyana.

Akshayamukthi: eternal salvation.

Akshāyani: undying

Akshi: existence, abode, possession, eye

Akshimanā: ruby

Akshita: yellow rice used by Hindus for worship and blessing.

Akshiti: that which is imperishable

Akupārā: free, independent

Ākuti: intention

Akutila: simple, straight-forward

5

Alaina: attractive, peaceful.

Alakā: trees, girl

Alaknandā: young girl, the celestial Ganga

Alambusa: an Apsara.

Alameda: popular tree.

Alametā: extremely intelligent

Alamelu: very sportive, extremely merry

Alana: light & buoyant, an offering, dear child

Alanda: variant of Alexandra, defender of mankind, helper

Alankara: decoration

Alanna: attractive, peaceful.

Ālāpini: a bite

Alarice: feminine of Alaric

Alba: highlands

Alberta: feminine of Albert

Albina: highlands

Alby: highlands

Alcina: strong-willed, persuasive

Alda: rich

Aldora: winged gift

Alekhya: painting, picture

Alena: light

Aletea: truth

Alexandra: defender of mankind, helper.

Alexis: helper, defender

Alfreda: feminine of Alfred

Alice: noble, truthful one

Alicia: truthful

Alida: Greek city in Asia minor

Alimā: wise, learned

Alin: sister of Night

Aliptha: neutral, unbiased

Alishā: stately, grand

Alison: truthful one.

Alissa: truthful

Aliya: to group

Āliyā: high, exalted

Aliza: joyous

Alka: girl with long beautiful hair, noble & brilliant

Allanā: fair

Allegra: cheerful

Alleron: eagles soaring

Allina: a form of helen

Alma: the Soul, with dark red lips, soul, spirit

Almas: diamond, dagger

Alocia: ocean of forgiveness

Aloka: cry of victory, praise, luster

Alpanā: glad, delighted

Alpha: the first letter of the Greek alphabet, the first (child)

Altthea: truthful, sincere, wholesome, healing

Alva: fair, blonde

Alvinā: noble friend

Alysha: princess of pink

Alysia: truthful

Alyssa: from the flower Alyssum

Alysse: truthful

Amabel: lovable

Amadea: feminine of Amadeo.

Amadi: rejoice, Sun god

Amalā: pure, shining, Lakshmi

Amalendu: full moon

Amanda: beloved, precious thing, worth loving, lovable

Amani: to wish for, greatful

Amara: imperishable, eternal beauty

Amaranganā: celestial damsel

Amaranth: from the flower Amaranth.

Amaraprabha: eternal shine

Amaravathi: name of Indra's kingdom

Amari: eternal

Amāris: child of the moon

Amartā: immortal

Amaryllis: from the flower Amaryllisbelladonna

Amati: beyond intellect, splendour, time, lustre

Amaya: the end

Ambā: mother, a god, woman

Ambālikā: mother, a sensitive person

7

Ambar: sky

Amber: precious stone, healing, one of the colours

Ambhini: water-born

Ambika: mother, compassionate, loving

Ambrosine: feminine of Ambrose

Ambruni: an Apsara's name

Ambu: arrow, water

Ambudha: cloud

Ambudhi: sea

Ambuja: lotus

Ambujakshi: lotus-eyed, with beautiful eyes

Amee: my friend

Amelia: industrious

Amena: honest

Amie: beloved, loved

Aminta: protector

Aminya: pure, chaste

Amira: princess, rich, grand

Amisha: guileless

Amita: truth, limitless

Amiti: boundless, divine

Amiya: nectar, full of tenderness

Amoda: happiness

Amodini: fragrance, famous

Amohanika: fragrance

Amogha: productive, unerring

Amorata: beloved

Amrakali: mango bud

Amramanjari: bunch of mango flowers

Amrapallavi: tender leaves of mango

Amrisha: genuine, real

Amrita: immortal, nectar-like, goddess

Amritamalini: with an everfresh garland, Durga

Amritavarshini: one who showers nectar

Amritha: deathless

Amrutha: nectar

Amruthakiran: cool rays, moonlight

Amruthamayi: full of sweetness

Amruthavarshini: one of the raagas (classical melody)

8

Amshu: a ray of light

Amshula: bright, radiant

Amshumala: a nymph, angel, apsara

Amshumathi: person with bright intellect, river Yamuna

Amtheshwari: eternal God

Amulya: priceless

Amy: loved, beloved

Ana: grace, favour

Anabelle: graceful and beautiful, of fire, Holy cow

Anabhra: clear-minded

Anadhika: without a superior

Anadya: immortal, divine, an apsara

Anaga: sinless, a river

Anala: without a blemish

Anamika: nameless yet full of virtues, ring finger

Anamra: humble, modest, propitious

Anan: clouds

Anandamayi: full of bliss

Anandana: happy

Anandhabhairavi: one of the ragas

Anandhalahari: wave of happiness

Anandhavardhini: one who increases happiness

Anandhitha: lady in joyous mood

Anandi: bestower of pleasure, Gauri

Ananga: love

Anangalekha: love letter

Anangamalini: God of love

Anangee: sexy

Ananta: eternal, divine

Anantasree (Ananthasri): who has boundless wealth

Anantika: simple

Anantya: without an equal

Ananya: sole, unique, peerless

Anapayina: eternal, Lakshmi

Anarghya: priceless

Anasuya: without envy or spite

9

Anatā: straight, erect

Ānati: modest, humble, respectful

Anatola: feminine of Anatole

Ānavi: kind, humane

Ancelin: hand-maiden

Anchiara: darkness falls

Anchita: honoured, worshipped

Andal (Aandal): devotee of Vishnu

Andie: strong

Andrea: lady Andrew feminine

Andreana: strong and womanly

Aneemā: wife of Lord Ganesh

Aneeshā: without night

Anemone: windflower

Angaja: daughter

Anganā: a beautiful woman

Angani: attractive girl

Angāritā: blossom of kinshuk tree, a river

Angeerā: celestial, divine, beyond description

Angel: messenger

Angela: angelic, messenger, heavenly messenger

Angelica: from the herb Angelica, like an angel

Angelina: angel, messenger.

Angira: mother of Brihaspati

Anguri: finger, ring finger

Anhati: gift

Anika: Goddess Durga

Anima: the power of becoming small

Anindā: beyond reproach

Anindita: one who cannot be defamed, blameless

Anisā: friendly

Anisha: continuous, without interruption, has an everlasting flame for eternity

Anitā: guileless, a leader, grace

Anitra: for the Arab girl in riegs peer gynt suite

Anjalā: unscorched

10

Anjali: hollow formed by joining hands together

Anjana: dusky, swarthy

Anjanam: night, fire, jet black

Anjashi: honest, not dark, deceitless

Anji: blesser

Anjini: blessed

Anjori: moonlight

Anju: one who lives in the heart

Anjum: a token, a signet, a star

Anjuna: name of Hanuman's mother

Ankita: with auspicious marks

Ankitha: a signet, symbol

Ankolika: personifier of love and respect

Ankur: a sprout

Ankushi: one who exercises restraint

Ann: gracious, a form of Hannah

Anna: graceful, variant of Hannah

Annabel: lovable

Annabelle: joy

Annada: godess of food, Parvathi

Annada: bestower of food, Durga

Annapurna: bestower of food to the utmost, Durga

Anne: favouring, grace, mercy

Annel: combination of Anna and Elena

Anneliese: graceful and consecrated to God

Annette: grace, mercy

Annie: favour, grace

Annise: pineapple

Annunciata: bearer of news

Anokhi: unique

Anoma: illustrious

Anona: the Roman goddess of crops

Anoona: perfect

Anora: grace and honor

Anouksha: endearment, fullfilment of desire

Anselma: feminine of Anselm

Anshu: sunbeam

Anshumaala: garland of rays

Anshumālā: halo, as glorious as the sun, a garland of rays

Anshumati: resplendent, wise, bearer of rays

Antara: second note in Hindusthani music

Anthahkarana: sympathy, kindness, tenderness

Anthea: flowerlike

Āntikā: elder sister

Antoinette: inestimable, without price, feminine form of Anthony

Antonia: feminine of Anthony

Anubhā: one who follows glory, lightning

Anubhuti: experience

Anuchārā: well behaved, an apsara, devoted to learning

Anugā: a companion, a follower, an apsara

Anugathadevi: a friend, a person who accompanies, a wife

Anugraha: blessings, grace

Anujā: younger sister

Anukā: backbone, support

Anukampa: sympathy, compassion

Anukampā: kindness, tenderness, pity

Anukeerthana: praising God's virtues

Anuksha: every moment

Anulā: gentle, tamed

Anulekha: beautiful picture

Anulekhā: a follower of destiny

Anuli: feminine of Anthony, respected, homage

Anuloma: sequence

Anumegha: following the rain

Anumita: logically established, analytical, precise

Anumloche: an apsara's name

12

Anumodita: delighted, applauded

Anūnā: superior, entire, an apsara

Anunaya: gentle, comfort

Anuneeta: learned, wise, respected

Anunita: prayer

Anupa: goddess Kali

Anupā: unique, unequalled, river bank

Anupallavi: tender, fragrant, young, soft like a petal, part of the song which is sung immediately after the pallavi (headlines of a song)

Anupamā: unique, matchless, rare

Anuprabha: brightness

Anupriya: one without comparison

Anura: attachment, love, compassion

Anuradha: one of the 27 stars

Anurādhā: bestower of welfare

Anuragha: love

Anuraghini: beloved

Anurakthi: love, affection

Anurakti: love, devotion, affection

Anurama: pretty, Lakshmi

Anuranjana: one who pleases the mind

Anuranjanā: love, affection

Anurati: consent

Anurimā: fond of, attached

Anurupa: suitable

Anusarā: full of desires

Anusha: name of a star, beautiful morning

Anusheela: good character

Anusheetha: to be calm

Anushma: without any heat

Anushobhini: shining, dignified, illuminant

Anushree: glorious, famous

Anushri: beautiful, pretty

Anusree: pretty, Lakshmi

Anusuya: wife of rishi

13

Anutā: gentle, agreeable

Anutānkshā: desire, wish

Anutara: unanswered

Anuvindha: one who receives

Anuvindā: discoverer, finder

Anuvrindha: Krishna's queen, Mitravinda's another name

Anvadhyā: goddess

Anvita: who bridges the gap

Anvitā: linked to, understood, reached by the mind

Anya: gracious.

Anyā: that which is not exhaustible

Anyi: her destiny

Aoife: beauty

Apaara: materialistic knowledge

Apala: most beautiful lady

Apārā: boundless, divine, unequalled

Aparaajita: unconquerable woman

Aparamitha: limitless

Aparnā: without leaves, Parvati

Aparanji: pure gold

Aparoopa: extremely beautiful woman, special, uncommon.

Apeksha: expectation, wish, desire

Apekshitā: desired, expected, awaited

Apoorva: special

April: opening, forthcoming, of the month April

Apsara: celestial maiden, heavenly woman, a fairy

Āpti: abundance, fortune, fulfilment

Apuroopa: extremely beautiful woman

Apurva: special

Apūrvā: incomparable, extraordinary

Aquaria: from aquarius, the constellation and Zodiacal sign

Ara: altar

Arabella: beautiful altar

Ārādhanā: worship, prayer

Ārādhitā: worshipped, a receiver of devotion

Aradhite: one who is worshipped

Aragili: parrot

Arajā: clean, pure, virtuous

Aranyani: Parvati, Goddess of vegetation

Ārati: offering prayer, spiritual, venerated

Aravalli: name of a hill

Aravinda: blue lotus

Aravindini: fragrant, beautiful, auspicious

Archanā: propitiated, worship

Archis: flame, illuminating, ray of light

Archisha: a ray of light

Archita: worshipped woman

Ardath: flowering field

Ardella: fervent

Arden: eagle valley

Ardis: fervent

Areta: virtuous

Areth: earth

Aretha: best

Argenta: silvery

Arhanā: honoured, worship, venerated

Arhantikā: worshipper, one who shuns violence

Aria: melody of an opera

Ariadne: chaste, holy

Ariadyna: came from the love

Ariana: holy song/singer/ voice, chaste, holy, like silver

Arianne: holyone

Ariba: intelligent, skillful, heights

Ariel: spirit of air or water, lion of God

Ariktā: satisfied, abundant

Ariprā: spotless, virtuous, divine

Arishṭṭā: safe, unhurt

Arisina: turmeric, auspicious yellow powder

Arjā: pure, virtuous, divine

Arkajā: daughter of sun god, river Yamuna

Arkavathi: a tributary of river Kaveri

Ārleen: pledge

Arlene: pledge

Armilla: bracelet

Armina: warrior maid

Arna: cedar

Ārohi: positive, progressive, ascending

Arpanā: auspicious, sacred, venerated

Arpita: dedicated

Arpitā: offered, delivered, entrusted, surrendered

Arpitaa: that which is offered

Artemis: Goddess of the hunt and the moon

Arthada: Lakshmi

Arthanā: entreaty

Arti(Aarti) Arati (Aarati): a ritual done on auspicious occasions

Artikā: elder sister

Arujā: daughter of Sun god

Arukshitā: not dry, supple, young, soft, tender

Aruna: dawn

Arunā: red, life-giving, passionate, an apsara

Arundati: wife of sage Vasistha, a morning star, Rudrakshi garland

Arundhati: fidelity

Aruni: ruddy, dawn, gold, passionate, illuminating, sacred

Arunikā: tawny red, bright, passionate

Arunimā: reddish glow, sacred dawn glow

Arūpā: formless, unbounded, divine

Arushi: first ray of the sun

Arva: fertile

Arvanti: nymph, mare

Arwa: wonderful, magnificent, marvellous

Āryā: a noble lady, worshipped, respected, baby Durga

Āryaki: honoured, respected, Durga

Aryama: respected lady

Aryamba: mother of Sri Sankaracharya

Āshā: desire, wish, space, region

Ashadeep: light of hope

Ashajyothi: light of hope

Ashakiran: ray of hope

Ashalatha: creeper of hope

Āshāli: liked by all

Ashanee: thunderbolt, lighting, supreme Goddess

Ashankitha: without fear or doubt

Ashapoornadevi: who has fulfilled the desire, full of hope

Ashavari: name of a raga

Ashcharya(Aashcharya): wonder

Āsheeshā: blessed, hope

Ashika(Aashika): beloved, desired, hope

Ashima: endless, limitless, without boundaries

Ashira: wealthy

Ashlee: ashtree meadow

Ashlesha: name of a star

Ashley: ash-tree, hope and helpful, meadow of ash trees

Ashmaki: strong and subtle

Ashna: daughter of Bali

Ashokā: without sorrow, blossom of Ashoka tree

Ashwabha: lightening

Ashwākiñi: strong, swift

Ashviktā: a small mare

Ashwini: wealthy, a swift mover

Asia: for the continent Asia

Asima: endless, limitless, without boundaries

Asita: river

Asitā: unbound, the dark one

Aslin: dream

Asmita: one with ego

Asmitā: renunciation

Aspasia: welcome

Āsthā: care, hope, support, confidence, consideration

Astra: star

Astrid: divine strength, divine power

Aswini: name of a star, female horse

Atalaya: watchtower

Atara: crown

Atefa: compassionate, kind

Athalia: god is mighty

Athena: the goddess of wisdom

Atianna: little princess

Atibālā: goddess

Atifa: compassionate, kind

Atiki: overflowing, excelling

Atimoda: very fragrant, very happy, jasmine

Atira: prayer

Atishaya: superiority, preeminence.

Atithi: guest

Atlanta: a huntress in Greek mythology

Attar: scent, fragrance

Atūhā: fragrant, jasmine

Atulya: unequalled

Ātyreji: receptacle of glory

Aubree: golden-haired queen of the spirit world

Auḍrey: noble, strength

Augusta: majestic, grand, feminine form of August

Aura: breeze, goddess of breeze

Aurelia: golden

Aurora: dawn

Autumn: ice princess, for the season

Ava: bird, birdlike

Avabhā: brilliant, bright

Avanati: humble, modest

Avani: earth

Avanji: daughter of earth, Seetha

Avanthi: name of a historical city

Avanti: endless, modest

Avantikā: very modest

Avatoda: name of a river in heaven

Avenā: oats

18

Avery: rules with elf wisdom

Avichalā: everlasting

Aviella: god is my father

Avinashini: eternal, imperishable

Avishi: not poisonous, heaven, earth, nectar-like

Avishyā: desire, full of ardour

Avital: dew of my father

Aviva: spring

Avoda: work

Ayah: bright

Ayala: gazelle

Ayanna: innocent, anything

Āyati: posterity, dignity, majesty

Astee: existed

Asthōlā: not fat

Atimoda: extremely delighted

Auchitee: appropriate

Avantee: modest, the name of the city

Ayeshā: Prophet Mohammed's favourite wife

Aylivia: unique, blessed or anointed

Ayodhikā: calm, peace-loving

Ayofemi: joy loves me, the joy of God is with me

Ayushi: long life

Azalea: from the flower Azalea

Azaleā: flower, democracy

Azela: helped by God

Aziza: beloved, precious, beautiful

Azizāh: beloved, precious, rare

Azura: sky-blue

Azusena: lily

Avarā: youngest.

Avishee: without poison ocean

Ayodhikā: peace, loving, calm.

Ayugoo: friendless.

B

Baako: first born

Babeṭte: consecrated to God

Babitā: born in the first quarter of an astrological day

Bachendri: sense of speech, tongue

Bādarāyaṇi: pure, young, new, perfume

Bāgeshree: beauty, prosperity

Bāhair: beautiful, delicate

Bahār: spring, beauty, glory

Bahati: fortunate

Bahudā: giving bountifully

Bahulikā: multiplied, manifold, magnified, a multifaceted personality

Bahumati: extremely knowledgeable, a scholar patient, watchful, circumspect

Bailey: steward, public official, courtyard with castle walls

Bakulā: like a crane, blossom of Bakula tree, patient, watchful, circumspect

Bakulikā: small blossom of Bakula tree

Bakulitā: decked with Bakula blossoms

Bala: daughter of Lalitha Parameshwari, who is always a nine year old girl

Bālā: girl, jasmine, young child

Baladā: bestower of strength

Balamani: gem among children

Bālasandhyā: early twilight, dawn

Bālini: strong, Ashwini, constellation

Bambi: little child, pet name

Bamini: shining, beautiful, radiant

Bandhini: binder, bond, bound

Bandhurā: charming, lovely

Barakhā: white one

Barbara: foreign, foreign land, strange

Barhiña: decked with peacock feathers

Basanthi: the spring season

Basanti: of the spring, excitement

Basaveshwari: goddess Parvathi

Basila: feminine of Basil

Basimā: smiling

Basudā: earth

Batami: daughter of my people

Bathilda: battle maid

Bathsheba: daughter of the oath

Batya: daughter of the God

Beata: happy, blessed one

Beatrice (Beatriz): she who brings joy

Becky: short form of Rebecca

Beenā: harp

Bekuri: playing a musical instrument, an apsara

Belā: jasmine creeper

Belen: bethlehem

Belenen: star of waters

Belicia: dedicated to God

Belinda: beautiful and pretty, beautiful girl

Bella: pledged to god, lovely one, fair

Belle: beautiful

Belli: companion

Benazir: matchless, with no equal, peerless

Benecia: blessed one

Benedicta: femenine of Benedict

Benigna: kind

Benita: blessed

Beniyāz: carefree, with no wants

Berdina: glorious

Berenice: one who brings victory

Berkeley: the birch tree meadow, where birches grow

Bernadette: feminine of Bernard, little strong bear

Bernadine: bold as bear

Berne: bold as bear

Bernice: one who brings victory

Bertha: bright, shining one

Bertina: bright

Beryl: a gem stone, from the gem Beryl

Bessy: consecrated to God, Elizabeth

Beth: a form of Elizabeth, consecrated to God

Bethea: name of maid servant of Jehovah

Bethel: house of God

Bethesda: house of mercy

Betsy: consecrated to God, Elizabeth.

Beṭṭinā: consecrated to God

Betty: a form of Elizabeth, consecrated to God

Beulā: married

Beulah: claimed as a wife, a name symbolic of the heavenly Zion, she who will marry

Beverly: name of a place, beaver stream, meadow dweller

Bhaanvee: the sun

Bhadrā: beautiful, fair, fortunate, prosperous, gentle, gracious, auspicious

Bhadrāvati: noble

Bhadrawathi: wife of King Pareekshit

Bhadrikā: a noble woman, virtuous, auspicious, beautiful

Bhāgavanti: fortunate, shareholder

Bhageerathi: river Ganga

Bhagya Lakshmi: goddess of wealth

Bhagyashree: goddess of fortune, Lakshmi

Bhairavi: Parvathi, one of the melodies in Classical music

Bhāmā: splendour, light

Bhāmini: radiant, beautiful, glorious

Bhānavi: shining like the sun, sacred, illuminating

Bhānu: light, beautiful, virtuous, enlightened

Bhānujā: daughter of Sun god

Bhānumati: luminous, famous, enlightening, beautiful

Bhānupriyā: beloved of Sun god

Bhānushree: as glorious as the sun

Bharaṇi: fulfiller

Bharathi: Saraswati, mother of India

Bharati: Saraswati

Bhāravā: pleasing sound, agile

Bhārgavi: descendant of Bhrigu, radiant, charming, beautiful, Lakshmi, Parvati

Bhāshi: bright, lustrous, illusory

Bhāswati: luminous, splendid

Bhāti: loved by all, splendour, perception, light, knowledge

Bhattarikā: noble lady, sacred, venerated, virtuous, Durga

Bhaumā: of the earth, steady

Bhavadā: giving life

Bhāvajā: boon of the heart, sentimental, sincere, beautiful, compassionate

Bhāvana: feeling, thought, meditation, feeling, imagination

Bhavāni: consort of Bhava, Parvati

Bhavanikā: living in a castle

Bhavanti: now, becoming, new, charming

Bhāviki: sentimental, emotional, real, natural

Bhāvilā: good, worthy

Bhāvini: inducing emotions, noble, beautiful, illustrious, sensitive, loving

Bhāvukā: sentimental, emotional, real, natural

Bhavyā: magnificent, beautiful, tranquil, worthy, Parvati

Bhavyakeerti: very wise, with magnificent fame

Bhogadā: bestower of worldly pleasures and happiness

Bhogavati: Ganga

Bhogyā: an object of enjoyment, precious stone

Bhomirā: from the earth, life-giving, tolerant

Bhoodevi: mother earth, Vishnus consort

Bhrāji: lustre, splendour, fame, glory

Bhramaramba: Parvathi

Bhrami: whirlwind, whirlpool

Bhūmayi: full of existence, from the earth

Bhumi: earth

Bhūmijā: born of earth, Sita

Bhumica: character, role, introduction

Bhūshā: ornament, precious, wealthy, much loved

Bhuvā: fire, earth

Bhuvanā: omnipresent, earth

Bhuvaneshwari: the earth

Bianca: fair, white, shining

Bibi: lady, wife

Bijali: lightening, active, electricity

Bijli: lightning, bright, illuminating, glorious

Billie: determination, strength

Bimbā: as glorious as the sun or moon

Bimbini: pupil (of the eye)

Bimla: vimala, pure

Bina: understanding

Bīnā: cute, melodious, harmonious

Bindhiya: dew drop, point

Bindiyā: a small dot

Bindu: mark, symbol, alphabet, truth, pearl, origin, subtle, absolute, divine, drop

Bindusree: dew drop, point

Binjal: goddess

Binotā: harp

Binti: daughter

Binty: daughter

Birdena: little bird

Birdie: bird

Birgitta: strong

Bisālā: sprout, bud, young, short, a child

24

Bithika: path between trees

Blaine: surname

Blair: field of battle

Blake: black

Blanche: fair, white

Bliss: joy, cheer, gladness

Blondell: fair-haired blonde

Blossom: flower, lovely

Bluebell: flower name

Bluma: flower like

Blythe: light hearted, joyful one

Bo: precious, a nickname

Bodhanā: the awakening, knowledge, intellect

Bonita: little good one, pretty

Bonnie: charming, good, pretty

Brāhmani: life of Brahma, wise, intelligent, sacred

Brandy: name of a beverage, sword, liquor

Branwen: white raven

Breanna: brianna

Breck: freckled

Bree: broth

Breena: fairy palace, raven maiden

Brenda: princess, fiery

Brenḍā: fiery hill, sword blade

Brennā: raven maid

Bretta: feminie of Bret

Breṭṭā: from Britain

Briana: feminine of Brian

Briānā: strong

Brianna: she ascends

Briar: a wild rose with prickly thorns

Brice: quick-moving

Bridgeṭ: resolute, strength, saint

Briean: strength

Brieṭṭa: strong

Brinā: protector

Brinda: Tulasi

Brindā: surrounded by many, Radha

Brinthadevi: queen of garden

Brionna: variant of Brianna

Briony: name of a flowering vine used in folk medicine

Brisa: the Greek name of the woman loved by Achilles

Brit: spotted, freckled

Britannia: from Britain

Briṭes: strength

Britt: strength

Bronwyn: white-breasted

Brook: stream

Bābhravee: fire clad

Bāgeshree: beauty, prosperity

Bāhulee: Kartik moon

Bāni: speech

Babhravee: Goddess Durga

Bahuta: plenty, cardamoms.

Bakulee: magnified

Bakulee: lady of the blossom

Brooke: dweller by the brook, water, stream

Brunella: brown-haired

Brunhilda: hereoine

Bryce: name of a saint

Bryn: hill

Bryna: hill place

Buena: good

Burḍeṭte: small bird

Byzanta: from the ancient city of Byzantium

Balajā: born of power, the earth

Bekuree: playing a musical instrument

Brrihadyuti: luminous

Brrihatee: heaven and earth

Brrinda: surrounded by many

Bulbul: a name of a bird

Bindu: drop

Brahantā: very strong, powerful

C

Caitlin: pure, variant of Katherine

Caitrin: form of Catherine

Caledonia: the old Latin name for Scotland

Calida: warm and loving

Calina: warm and loving

Calista: most beautiful

Calla: from the African plant, the calla lily

Callum: dove

Calvina: feminine of Calvin

Cambria: the Latin name for Wales

Cameo: a carved gem

Camillā: freedom girl

Camille: free-born, noble, young ceremonial attendant

Cammie: a short form of Camille

Camryn: crooked nose, awesome, energetic, excited, bent nose

Canace: child of the wind

Candice: an ancient hereditary title used by the Ethiopian queens

Candida: pure, bright

Capri: for a child born under the sign of Capricorn

Cara: beloved

Carensa: love

Carita: charitable

Carla: feminine form of Carl

Carletta: strong and womanly

Carley: feminine form of Charles

Carlota: petite or feminine

Carlottā: strong

Carmel: god's vineyard

Carmem: garden

Carol: joyous song

Caroline: feminine of Charles

Carolyne: feminine form of Charles

Carrie: little and womanly

Cary: honest, shy

Caryn: pure

Carys: love

Caryus: to love

Casey: brave, watchful

Cass: herald of peace

Cassandra: helper of men, the Trojan prophetess, unheeded prophetess

Cassaundra: a prophetess for humankind

Cassie: star light, star bright

Casta: pious

Catalina: pure

Catherine: pure

Catlina: pure

Catriona: pure

Cecilia: blind

Cecily: love and happy, blind

Celeste: celestrial, heavenly

Celia: blind

Celina: moon

Ceres: the Roman Goddess of the harvest

Cerise: cherry

Cerys: to love

Chāhanā: desire, affection

Chāhat: desire

Chaitāli: of the mind, with a sharp memory

Chaitri: born in spring, tender and fresh like a new blossom, ever-happy

Chakore: shining, content, a bird

Chakrikā: Lakshmi

Chakshani: illuminating to the eyes, illuminating

Chameli: jasmine

Champā: soothing, flower of the champaka tree

Champikā: small champa blossom

Chanasyā: delighting

Chanchalā: restless, lightning, a river, Lakshmi

Chanda: one of the names assumed by Sakti, the great Goddess

Chandā: passionate, wrathful, moon

Chandalikā: Durga

Chandanā: sandalwood, fragrant, cool, auspicious

Chandaneekā: a small sandalwood tree

Chandini: moonlight

Chandikā: Durga

Chāndini: silver, moonlight, cool, luminous, fair

Chandrā: moon

Chandrabālā: daughter of Moon god, as beautiful as the moon

Chandrabindu: crescent moon

Chandrahāsā: with a beautiful smile

Chandrajā: daughter of Moon god, moonbeam

Chandrajyoti: moonlight

Chandrakāntā: wife of Moon god

Chandrakriti: moon-shaped

Chandrāli: moonbeam

Chandramālā: garland of the moon, of great beauty, aura of the moon

Chandramathi: name of Harishchandra's wife

Chandrāni: wife of Moon god

Chandraprabhā: moon-beam

Chandrasheelā: stone of the moon, calm, soothing

Chandrashree: divine moon, tranquil, beautiful, charming

Chandrashubhrā: lit by the moon, as fair as the moon

Chandratārā: moon and stars conjoined, eye-catching

Chāndri: moonlight, cord, soothing, fair

Chandrikā: moonlight, illuminant, cool, soothing, jasmine creeper

Chandrimā: moonlight

Chāndvati: Durga

Chanel: name of a famous perfume

Chanmundeswari: Durga

29

Chantal: stony place

Chantelle: song

Charchitā: repeating a word, fragrant, attractive

Charaṇi: wanderer, a bird

Charissa: grace, kindness

Charity: esteem

Charlene: strong, womanly

Charlese: princess

Charlotte: feminine of Charles

Charmaine: little song

Charshani: active, swift, moonlight, saffron, intelligence

Chāru: beautiful

Chāruchitrā: beautiful

Charukeshi: one with beautiful hair

Chārulatā: beautiful vine

Charumathi: one with beautiful mind

Chārumati: wise, intelligent, enlightened

Chārunetrā: with beautiful eyes

Chārusheelā: beautiful jewel

Chārutamā: most beautiful

Chāruvāki: with a sweet tongue, pleasant

Chāruveṇi: a beautiful braid

Chāruvi: splendour

Chārvāngi: with a beautiful body

Chaturi: clever, skilful, wise

Chaturikā: clever, skilful

Chausiku: born at night

Chava: life-giving

Chhavi: reflection, image, ray of light, image, splendour

Chhāyā: shade, shadow, reflection, beauty, colour, shine, likeness

Chelanā: of consciousness nature

Chellryn: earth witch

Chelsea: river, landing place

Chelsi: name of a place

Chenoa: white dove

Cher: beloved, dear

Cherie: dear one

Cheryl: feminine of Charles

Chetaki: perceptible, jasmine

Chetana: intelligence, consciousness, wisdom, life, knowledge, sense

Cheyenne: a tribal name

Chintamani: a gem which is believed to give whatever asked

Chiquitta: little one

Chitpara: beyond thought, indescribable

Chitra: beautiful, picture, ornament, sky, painting, heaven, worldly illusion, conspicuous, an apsara

Chitrajyoti: luminous, shining brightly

Chitrakala: arts of eternal knowledge

Chitralekha: beautiful picture, friend of Urvashi, friend of Usha

Chitrali: wonderful woman, friend of the strange

Chitramaya: worldly illusion, strange manifestation

Chitramayi: full of wonders, like a picture

Chitrangi: with a charming body

Chitrani: Ganga

Chitrashree: with divine beauty

Chitravati: decorated

Chitrini: endowed with excellence, talented, brightly ornamented

Chitrita: ornamented, painted

Chitta: intellectual, spiritual, thoughtful

Chitti: thought, understanding, devotion

Chloe: fertile, young maiden, goddess of agriculture, blooming, young green shoot

Chloie: variant of Chloe

Chloris: the Goddess of flowers

Choodamani: jewel worn on head

31

Christabelle: beautiful Christian

Christina: follower of Christ, annointed

Christinna: follower of Christ, annointed

Christean: feminine form of Christian

Christine: feminine of Christian

Chudalā: forming the crest, an apsara

Chumbā: kiss, adorable person

Ciana: feminine form of John

Ciara: dark

Cicely: from a Roman clan name

Cierra: black

Cindrella: from the fairy tale

Clair, Clare: bright, shining

Claire: clear, bright, brilliant

Clara: bright, shining

Clarabelle: bright and beautiful

Clare: clear, shinning

Clareta: clear, bright, brilliant

Clarissa: made famous

Claudia: feminine of Claudius, dame

Clelia: a legendary Roman heroine

Clematia: vine

Clementine: feminine of Clement

Cleopatra: of a famous father

Clorinda: a name coined by the Italian poet Tasso

Clothilda: battle maid

Clover: from the flower clover

Clytie: splendid

Cody: helpful

Colette: victorious

Colleen: girl

Columba: dove

Columbia: dove

Comfort: aid, comfort

Conception: beginning

Concordia: harmony

Connie: a familar form of Constance

Consolata: consolation

Constance: constancy, firmness.

Consuela: consolation

Cora: maiden

Corabelle: beautiful maiden

Coral: sea coral

Cordelia: jewel of the sea

Coretta: maiden

Corin: lion

Corinnā: maiden

Corinne: maiden

Corinthia: from the Greek city of Corinth

Corliss: cheerful and generous

Cornelia: feminine of Cornelius

Corryn: lion

Cosima: feminine of Cosmo

Courtney: courtly, courteous.

Cressida: golden

Crispina: feminine of Crispin

Crysella: dark beauty

Crystal: brilliant, pure, ice, bright

Curyn: lion

Cy: baby girl

Cynara: perhaps from the Aegean island of Zinara

Cynthia: a greek God, the Goddess of the Moon

Cypria: from the island of Cyprus

Cyra: feminine of Cyrus

Cyrena: the water nymph

Cyril: from god

Cyrilla: feminine of Cyril

Cytherea: a title assigned to Venus from the island of Cythera, her supposed birthplace

D

Dacia: from the Roman province of Dacia

Daeya: fae Magic

Daffodil: from the flower daffodil, name of a flower

Dafna: laurel

Dagmar: joy of the Danes

Dahlia: from the flower dahlia, name of a flower

Daisy: eye of the day

Ḍaisy: pearl, flower

Daksahyani: Parvati, daughter of Daksha

Dakshā: earth

Dakshakanyā: an able daughter

Dakshata: skill

Dakshāyaṅi: emerging from fire, golden ornament, daughter of a perfect being

Dakshayi: perfect

Dakshiṇā: donation to priest or god, able, fit, right-handed

Dakshinya: modesty

Dalajā: honey, produced from petals

Ḍale: valley

Dalia: branch

Dalila: gentle

Dalini: Durga

Dallas: from the city in Texas

Dāmā: suppressor, wealthy, self-restrained

Damalis: conqueror

Damara: gentle

Damati: conquering

Damayanthi: queen of Nala

Damayanti: self-restrained, subduer of men

Dāmini: lightning

Damita: young lady

Dampā: lightning

Dana: feminine of Daniel, mother of Gods in myths, from Denmark

Danah: cheerfulness, pearl, shouts of joy, song, pride, presumption

Danda: combination of Danny and Linda

Danee,Danay,Denay: name of the Mother of Perseus by Zeus

Danette: feminine form of Daniel

Danica: morning star

Daniela: feminine of Daniel

Danielle: harmony, love, feminine form of Daniel, God is my judge

Danika: morning star

Danita: God is my judge

Danna: feminine form of Daniel

Dānti: patience, self-restraint

Danu: high-pitched

Daphine: laurel tree

Ḍaphne: laurel

Dara: house of wisdom

Darcie: from the fortress

Darda: pearl of wisdom

Dardanella: from the Dardanelles, the straits seperating Europe and Asia

Darice: feminine of Darius

Darie: of unique origin, originality

Darika: maiden

Darlene: dear one, little darling

Darpana: mirror, looking glass

Darpañikā: a small mirror

Darshana: religious text, vision

Darshanā: intellect, virtue

Darshani: one who is worth looking at, another name of Durga

Darshatashree: of apparent beauty

Darshayāmini: night worthy of watching, new-moon night

Darshini: worth looking at, Durga

Darshita: good morning

Dashahara: river Ganga

Dashami: 10th day of paksha in Hindu Calendar

Dattādevi: goddess of gifts

Datti: a gift

Davana: a fragnant herb, used to worship

Davani: fire

Davida: feminine of David

Davina: beloved, feminine form of David

Davini: lightning

Dawn: break of day

Dayā: compassion, sympathy

Dayamayi: kind hearted, compassionate person

Dayanā: compassionate

Dayānvitā: surrounded by mercy, full of mercy

Dayitā: worthy of compassion, beloved, cherished

Dayitha: beloved

Deana: feminine of Dean

Deanara: goddess of beauty

Deanna: divine, sunshine

Debbie: bee

Deborah: queen bee

Decembra: from the month December

Decima: the tenth (child)

Deeksha: a pledge, dedication, religious initiation

Deepā: illuminated, enlightening

Deepadhari: river Ganga, an angel

Deepākshi: bright-eyed

Deepāli: a row of lights

Deepanā: illuminating, kindler, in flames, passion

Deepāni: exciting, stimulating, illuminating

Deepānjali: a prayer lamp

Deepavati: earth

Deepikā: a small lamp, light, moonlight

Deepamale: river Ganga, an angel

Deepanjali: express dedication by lamps

Deeparathi: a ritual done with lamps on auspicious occasion.

Deepika: small lamp

Deepshikhā: flame of lamp

Deeptā: illuminated, blazing, bright, brilliant

Deepthi: glow, shine

Deepti: radiance, brightness, enlightening, illuminating

Deeraghikā: tall girl, oblong lake

Delanah: noble protector

Delaney: dark challenger

Delia: a title for Artemis, the moon Goddess

Delicia: delightful

Delilah: brooding

Delmara: from the sea

Delphine: from the flower delphinium

Demetria: from Demeter, Goddess of fertility

Demi: half

Dena: vindicated

Denise: follower of Dionysus, the god of wine, Greek God.

Denye: follower of Dionysus, the god of wine, feminine of Dennis

Deonna: variant of Diana, divine

Derora: freedom

Deshnā: gift, offering

Desiree: desired, longed for

Desma: vow, pledge

Destiny: fate

Devaduni: Ganga

Devagiri: divine knowledge

Devaki: divine, pious, glorious

Devala: a goddess

Devalatā: double jasmine

Devalekhā: divine line, celestial beauty

Devamālā: divine garland, an apsara

Devamani: kousthub the gem worn by Vishnu

Devamati: godly-minded, virtuous, venerated

Devanandā: joy of the gods, an apsara

Devangana: river Ganga, an angel

Devasena: a daughter of Daksha

Devashree: divine goddess, Lakshmi

Devasmita: with a divine smile

Devata: music personified

Devatha: goddess

Devavarnini: daughter of Bharadwaj

Devavathi: a Gandharva's daughter

Devayani: chariot of the gods, endowed with divine powers, divine affluence

Devayoni: divine creation

Deveshi: chief of the goddesses, Durga

Devi: goddess, wife

Devika: Yudhishtra's wife

Devona: from Devon

Deya: in the shadow she moves

Dhairya: patience, calmness

Dhamini: pipe, tube

Dhanada: bestowing wealth

Dhanarati: containing wealth

Dhanashree: goddess of wealth

Dhanishttha: dwelling in wealth, very wealthy

Dhanu: sage Kashyap's wife

Dhanvanya: oasis, jungle treasure

Dhanya: virtuous, bestowing wealth, good

Dhanyatha: success, fulfillment

Dhara: supporter, earth, a gold mass

Dharani: holding, possessing, bearing

Dharathi: earth

Dharini: earth, a star, the globe

Dharithri: earth

Dharmini: pious, religious, virtuous, perfume

Dhatreyika: supporter, nurse, companion

Dhathri: earth

Dhaula: white

Dhavala: immaculate, white

Dheeptha: Lakshmi

Dheerata: courage, heroism

Dheeshana: vessel for soma, knowledge, speech, hymn, intelligence

Dhenu: cow

Dhenuka: milch cow

Dhenumathi: another name of river Gomathi

Dhiksha: initiation, consecration, dedication

Dhita: a daughter

Dhiti: idea, wisdom, reflection, intention, prayer

Dhoolika: dew drop

Dhoothapapa: a river

Dhritavati: calm, steady, a river

Dhriti: firmness, constancy, joy, resolution

Dhritimati: resolute, steadfast

Dhruti: earth

Dhruvatara: pole star, star with everlasting radiance

Dhūlikā: pollen of flowers

Dhun: wealth

Dhuti: splendour, majesty, lustre, light

Dhyana: contemplation, meditation

Dhyeyā: ideal, aim

Diamanta: like a diamond

Diana: divine, the goddess of the hunting and the nature

Diane: the Roman goddess of the moon and the hunt

Diantha: from the flower dianthus

Dido: the legendary queen of Carthage

Digdevatha: diety presiding over the night

Dilan: love

Diljot: light of the heart

Dilys: feminine of Dylan

Dinah: the judged

Dinika: sun

Dinumati: Gomati river

Dione: the mother of Aphrodite

Dipakalika: flame of a lamp

Dipakshit: bright-eyed

Dipali: a row of lights

Dipna: glitter, shine

Dipra: radiant, shining, flaming

Dipti: lightning

Disha: direction, region

Dishtti: direction, auspicious, good fortune, joy

Diti: glow, splendour, light, brightness, beauty

Divija: born of the sky, celestial, heaven-born, goddess

Divya: divine, charming, heavenly, celestial

Divyagandha: with divine fragrance

Divyajyoti: divine light

Divyakriti: of divine form, beautiful

Divyamabari: sky, one without finest clothes

Divyangani: an angel, celestial being

Divyasaritha: river Ganga

Dixie: girl of the south

Diya: deepa, lamp

Diza: joy

Dochilla: gentle, teachable

Dodi: beloved, beloved friend

Dolly: gift of God

Dolores: from Virgin Mary, sorrows.

Doloris: sorrowful, a name for the Virgin Mary

Dominica: the lords

Donalda: feminine of Donald

Donata: gift

Donna: lady, mistress of the house, housewife

Dora: gift

Dorcas: golden

Dorinda: beautiful gift

Doris: name of a place, of the sea

Dorothy: gift of God

Ḍory: golden-haired

Dorya: gods generation

Dova: feminine of Dov

Dove: a bird

Draupadi: daughter of Drupada, Pandava's wife

Drishikā: good looking

Druhi: daughter

Drupanandini: Draupadi

Drusilla: soft-eyed

Druti: softened, tender

Duā: blessing, benediction

Duana: little dark girl

Dulāri: lovable

Dulcie: sweet

Dwāpara: a friend of Kali

Dwipā: female elephant

Dwipādee: with two legs

Dyvomayee: full of splendour

Dumati: with bright intellect, a river

Dureshwari: goddess

Durgā: unapproachable, goddess of the universe

Durvaswati: offering worship, enjoying worship

Dwan: richly dark

Dyotanā: illuminating rays, shining

Dyotani: splendour, brightness

Dyukshā: celestial

Dyumani: shining gem, the sun

Dyumayi: full of brightness

Dyuthi: shining, bright

Dyuvadhū: celestial woman, an apsara

Dzifa: my heart is at peace, peaceful heart

Dyotanā: illuminating

Dyotinee: splendour

Dyuti: splendour

Doorvā: panic

E

Earlene: noblewoman

Eartha: the earth

Eashaa: desire, Durga

Eashana: desire

Eashani: goddess Parvathi

Eashanye: the diety who looks after the direction · Eashanya (East)

Eashita: wanted, superiority

Eashtadevata: favourite diety

Eashwari: goddess Parvathi

Easter: related to Easter

Ebbani: dew drops

Ebony: dark beauty

Eccha: desire

Ecchita: wanted

Ecchumati: river

Echo: the nymph who loved Narcissus

Eda a: fire, fiery one, flame, ardent.

Eḍānā: zealous, fiery

Eḍḍā: rich

Eden: delight

Edhā: prosperity, joy

Edith: rich gift

Edlyn: noble one

Edmunda: feminine of Edmund

Edna: rejuvenation

Eḍonā: rejuvenation

Edor a: fire, fiery one, flame, ardent

Edra: powerful

Edrie: powerful

Edsel: rich

Edwarda: feminine of Edward

Eḍwinā: feminine form of Edwin

Eeswari: another name of Lalithamba

Efimia: happiness

Efrona: feminine of Efron

42

Egberta: feminine of Egbert

Eglantine: wild rose

Eileen: variant of Helen

Eirean: silver

Eka: one and only, matchless, firm, Durga

Ekachandrā: the only moon, the best one

Ekaja: only child

Ekākini: alone

Ekamati: concentrated

Ekananga: Krishna's sister, Yashoda's daughter

Ekānanshā: new moon

Ekangikā: of sandalwood, auspicious, frequent, fair, dear to the gods

Ekanta: beautiful, devoted to one

Ekāntikā: devoted to a single intention

Ekaparña: single-leafed, residing on a leaf

Ekapatala: sister of Parvathi, wife of sage Jaigeesghavya

Ekatha: unity

Ekavali: a necklace, daughter of king Raibhya

Ekāvali: a string of pearls

Ekisha: one goddess, primal goddess

Ekoparna: sister of Parvathi, wife of sage Asita

Ekshikā: eye

Ekta: unity

Ekyastikā: single string of pearls

Elā: earth, born of earth

Ela Devi: earth

Elaine: a form of Helen

Elana: oak tree

Elba: for the island off the coast of Italy

Eldrida: wise counselor

Eleanore: light

Electra: shining one

Elena: bright girl

Eleni: torch, light

Eliana: God's answer

Eliora: God is my light

Elisa: dedicated to God

Elise: another form of Elizabeth

Elissa: beautiful, regal, in control

Elizabeth: consecrated to God

Ella: light, short form of Eleanor and Ellen

Ellā: beautiful

Ellen: light, variant of Helen (shining light)

Ellice: feminine of Elias or Ellis

Ellie: beauty

Elma: feminine of Elmo

Elodra: golden, glided

Eloise: variant of Louise

Elokshi: hair black as cardamom creeper

Elsa: consecrated to God

Elvā: elf

Elvira: elfin

Elvisa: feminine of Elvis

Elysia: place where happy souls dwell, mythical place after death for heros

Ema: short form of Emily, flatterer, industrious, feminine form of Emil

Emani: trustworthy

Emelyn: combination of Emma and Lynn

Emerald: from the gem emerald

Emily: industrious, striving, artistic

Emina: distinguished

Emma: whole, complete, short form of Emily, flatterer, industrious

Emmanuela: feminine of Emmanuel

Emmy: flatterer

Emuna: faith

Enā: doe, black antelope

Ēnākshi: doe-eyed

Enam: God's gift

Endora: fountain

Ēni: deer, spotted, flowing stream

Enid: pure

Enrica: feminine of Enrico

Eona: female version of Ian

Erakā: hard grass

Erica: brave, ever powerful, victorious, ruler forever, femine of Eric

Erikā: ever powerful

Erin: peace

Erina: from Ireland

Erma: strong

Ernestine: feminine of Ernest

Eshā: desire, wish, intention

Eshañikā: fulfilling desire, goldsmith's balance

Eshikhā: achiever of objective, arrow, dart

Eshitā: wanted, yearning

Eshtartha: desired

Esinam: God has heard my cry

Esme: emerald, esteemed

Esmereldā: green gemstone

Estelle: star

Esther: star

Etā: shining, flowing

Etahā: shining

Ethaniel: a mother's light and sun

Ethel: noble

Eti: arrival

Etta: star

Eudocia: respected

Eudora: generous gift

Eugenia: well born

Eulaliā: fair of speech

Eunice: joyful, victorious

Euphemia: of good reputation

Euphrata: from the river Euphrates

Europa: from the continent of Europe

Eurydice: the wife of Orpheus

Eustacia: feminine of Eustace

Euxina: from the Euxine, black sea

Eva: lifegiving

Evadnā: fortunate

Evangelia: one who brings good news

Evangeline: bearer of good news

Eve: life-giving

Evelina: life-giving

Evelinā: youth

Evelyn: lively, pleasant

Evie: living one

Ezara: feminine of Ezra

F

Fabiana: feminine of Fabian

Faiha: expanse, aromatic, perfumed

Faihah: perfume, fragrance

Fainan: one with luxurious hair

Faith: belief, loyalty

Faiza: successful

Fakeeha: cheerful

Fakhira: splendid, elegant

Fakhr: pride

Fakhta: dove

Falaq: sky

Falna: famous, prosper

Fanchon: of Frances

Fancy: imagination

Fanhana: female artist

Fanny: feminine of Francis

Fanya: free

Faqiha: well-versed in law, theologian

Fara: top, head, head of a family

Farah: joy, happiness, gaiety

Farahan: gladly, cheerfully

Farhana: happy

Farahat: liveliness, ingenuity, nimbleness, swiftness, sprightliness

Farana: famous, glorious

Fareeda: wife

Fareena: wise, intelligent, one who brings good news

Farhat: happiness

Farida: sole, different, large pearl

Farihan: happy, woman

Farilata: betel leaf

Farrah: beautiful, wild ass

Farria: the storm preceeds her

Farya: friend

Farzi: queen (in chess, game)

Farzin: wise, intelligent, chess queen

Fasāh: shining in splendour

Fasanā: tale, myth, famous

Fasika: happiness

Fatāt: a young maid

Faten: pretty one

Fatimā: Prophet Muhammed's daughter

Fatin: captivating

Faustine: feminine of Faust

Fawn: young deer

Fay: fairy

Fayola: lucky

Fazanā: intelligent

Femi: love me

Felda: field

Felicia: happy, feminine form of Felix

Fenella: white-shouldered

Fern: feather

Fernanda: feminine of Ferdinand

Ffion: foxglove

Fidelia: faithful

Fidelity: faithfullness

Fifi: feminine of Joseph

Filiz: a flower, a tendril

Filomena: beloved, variant form of Philomena

Fiona: white

Firoza: turquoise

Firzan: chess queen

Fisa: peacock

Flavia: yellow

Fleta: swift

Fleur: flower

Flora: flowering

Florida: from the American state

Flossie: flowering

Flower: bloom

Fola: honorable

Fonda: foundation

Foolrani: flower queen

Forsythia: a small, yellow, bell-shaped flower (that grows on a shrub)

Fortune: destiny

Francesca: free

Frashmi: prosperity

Frayashti: worship, praise

Frea: lady

Frederica: feminine of Frederick

Freya: the goddess of fruitfulness

Freyā: dear, beloved

Freyanā: cherished

Frieda: feminine of Fredrick

Friedā: peace

Fritzie: feminine of Fritz

Frohar: angel

Fronde: leafy branch

Fulmati: goddess

Fulnā: gladden, to make one proud

Fulvia: golden

G

Gabhasti: ray, moonbeam, sunbeam

Gabrielle: feminine of Gabriel

Gagandeepika: lamp of the sky, sun

Gagansindhu: celestial Ganga, ocean of the sky

Gaia: an earth goddess

Gail: gay, lively

Gaja Lakshmi: godess Lakshmi (one of the 8 Lakshmis)

Gajra: garland of flowers

Galadriel: name of the queen of the elves

Galatea: ivory-colored

Gale: my father rejoices, delightful, source of joy

Gali: fountain

Galilea: from the province of Galilee

Galina: variant of Helen

Galya: god has redeemed

Gamati: with a flexible mind

Gambhari: sky-reaching

Gamin: with a graceful gait

Gamma: the third (child)

Gandha: fragrant

Gandhaja: of fragrant perfume

Gandhalata: fragrant creeper

Gandhali: perfumed

Gandhalika: fragrant, an apsara

Gandharika: preparing perfume

Gandharvi: speech of celestial

Gandhavadhu: fragrant maiden

Gandhavaruni: with perfumed juice

Gandhavati: sweetly scented, earth, wine

Gandhini: fragrant

Ganga: swift flowing

Gangika: like the Ganga, pure like the Ganga

Ganit: garden

Ganjan: excelling, conquering, surpassing

Gannika: counted of value, jasmine

Garda: protected

Gardenia: from the flower gardenia

Gargi: water-holding vessel, churn

Garima: grace, sublimity, divinity, greatness

Garlanda: wreath

Garnet: from the gem garnet

Gathika: song

Gauhar: pearl

Gaunika: jasmine, valuable

Gaurangi: fair, the colour of cow

Gauri: fair, brilliant, beautiful, jasmine

Gaurika: like Gauri, Shiva

Gautami: dispeller of darkness, name of a river

Gavah: stars of heaven

Gavrila: feminine of Gabriel

Gayantika: singing

Gayatri: *Vedic* mantra or chant

Gayatrini: the singer of the *Sama Veda* hymns

Gayla: festive party

Gayle: festive party

Gayne: woman

Gayora: valley of light

Gazit: of hewn stone

Geera: speech, song, *Vedic* hymn, voice, language, Saraswati

Geeradevi: goddess of speech

Geeta: song, poem, lyric

Geetali: as pure as the words of the *Geeta* or *Gita*

Geetanjali: devotional offering of a hymn

Geetashree: the divine *Gita*

Geeti: song

Geetikā: a short song

Gelyanda: wandering Angel

Gema: gem, jewel

Gemina: from the astrological sign Gemini

Gemma: gem, bud

Genesis: new beginning

Geneva: juniper tree

Genevieve: white wave

Georgia: feminine of George

Geraldine: feminine of Gerald

Geranium: from the flower geranium

Gerda: guarded, protected

Germaine: a German

Georgia: farmer

Gerogiana: feminine of George

Gertrude: spear maiden

Geshā: singer

Geula: redemption

Ghanānjani: with colleriums as black as the clouds, Durga

Ghanavallikā: creeper of the clouds, lightning

Ghazal: lyric poem

Ghoshā: resounding, fame, proclamation

Ghoshīnī: famed, proclaimed

Ghūrnikā: one who whirls

Gibralta: from the colony of straits of Gibraltar

Gila: joy

Gilada: my joy is eternal

Gilberta: feminine of Gilbert

Gilḍā: God's servant

Gili: my joy

Gillian: youthful

Gimra: fulfilled

Gina: garden, queen

Ginger: maidenly

Giovanna: feminine of Giovanni

Giribālā: daughter of the mountain, Parvati

Giridevi: Saraswati

Girijā: daughter of the mountain

Girikā: mountain summit

Girikarnī: mountain lotus

Girikamīkā: earth, mountains as vessels for seeds

Girimallikā: mountain creeper, a flower

Girinandini: daughter of the mountain, Parvati, Ganga

Girindramohini: beloved of the lord of the mountains, Parvati

Gireeshā: lady of the mountains, Parvati

Gireshmā: summer

Girisutā: daughter of the mountain, Parvati

Girni: praise, celebrity

Giselle: pledge

Gita: song, poem, line

Gitāli: lover of song

Gitana: gypsy

Gitanjali: collection of poems

Giulia: an Italian version of Julia

Giva: hill

Gladys: feminine of the Latin Claudius

Glenda: feminine of Glenn

Glendine: valley

Glenna: feminine of Glenn, valley

Gloria: glory

Gloriana: glory and grace

Gnaneswari: Saraswati

Goda: name of a devotee of Vishnu

Godāvari: granting water, bringer of prosperity, a river

Godetā: name of a flower

Gojā: born amidst rays, born in the earth

Goldie: gold

Gomati: rich in cattle, milky, a river

Gomedā: respecter of cows, beryl

Gopabālā: daughter of a cowherd

Gopajā: daughter of a cowherd

Gopāli: protector of cows, cowherdess, an apsara

Gopi: herdswoman, milkmaid of Krishna

Gopikā: herdswoman, cow protector, Radha

Gorochanā: yellow pigment, beautiful and virtuous woman

Gowri: Parvati

Grace: grace

Grashiā: flavour, grace

Greer: feminine of Gregory

Greta: a pearl

Gretchen: pearl

Gretel: pearl

Grihini: mistress of the house

Griselda: grey heroine

Guadalupe: wolf valley

Gulfroze: beautiful like a flower

Gudia: doll

Gudrun: daughter of the king of Nibelungs

Guinevere: white wave, white phantom, fair lady

Gulikā: anything round, a pearl

Gulmini: a creeper, clustering

Gulnār: pomegranate flower

Guñajā: daughter of virtue

Guñamayā: endowed with virtues

Guñāvarā: virtuous, meritorious, an apsara

Guñavati: virtuous

Guñaveeñā: virtuous

Guñchā: blossom, bud

Guñchalā: bunch of flowers

Guñitā: virtous, proficient

Gunjan: humming, a cluster of flowers

Gunjikā: humming, meditation

Gumñikā: well woven, garland, necklace

Gupti: protecting, preserving

Gurit: feminine of Gurice

Gurñikā: wife of a teacher

Gūrti: praise, approval

Garuda: guru-given

Gurudeepa: lamp of the grace

Gurumeeta: friend of the guru

Gurusharna: in the guru's protection

Gurwanti: virtuous, talented

Gāthā: story

Gabhasti: light

Gajata: a wreath of flower

Ganika: an astrologer

Gaveshna: search

Geerna: fame

Geeshee: celebrity

Geeti: singing, a song

Gustava: feminine of Gustave

Guyna: woman

Gwen: white, fair

Gwendolen: white-browed

Gwynne: white, fair

Gypsy: wanderer

Goshthi: conservation

Gorma: Goddess Parvati

Gullika: pearl

Guncha: blossom

Gunita: virtuous

Guniyal: a woman full of virtues

Gunja: daughter of virtue

H

Habibah: beloved

Hadara: splendid

Hadassah: myrtle tree

Hagar: one who flees

Haifa: slender

Hailie: gorgeous, funny

Haima: of the snow, golden, Parvati, Ganga

Haimavati: possessor of snow

Haimi: golden

Hairanyavati: possessing gold

Hala: earth, liquor, water, a female friend

Halcyone: kingfisher bird

Haldis: purposeful

Haleh: eclipse

Halipriya: beloved of Vishnu

Haley: ingenious, scientific, ingenious

Halima: gentle

Hallie: feminine of Harold

Halona: happy fortune

Hameeda: praiseworthy

Hamna: warm hearted

Hamra: red, fair lady

Hamsa: swan, soul, goose, gander

Hamsika: goddess Saraswati

Hamuda: desirable

Hanan: mercy

Hanifa: true

Hannah: grace, god has favoured me, favouring, mercy, mother of Samuel

Hansagamini: as graceful as a swan

Hansanadini: slender-waisted, graceful gait, cuckoo-voiced

Hansanandini: daughter of a swan

Hansaveni: swan-like braid, with a beautiful braid, Saraswati

Hansi: swan

Hansika: swan

Hansini: swan, goose

Hanum: woman, maiden

Haralda: feminine of Harold

Haramālā: garland of Shiva

Harapriyā: beloved of Shiva, Parvati

Hārāvali: garland of pearls

Hardikā: sincere

Hari: reddish-brown, tawny

Haribālā: daughter of Vishnu

Haridrā: turmeric

Harika: another name for Goddess Lakshmi, dear to Lord Vishnu

Harikāntā: dear to Vishnu, Lakshmi

Harikinā: engrossed in Hari

Harileenā: merged in Vishnu

Harimālā: garland of Vishnu

Harinākshi: doe-eyed

Harini: doe, gazelle, green, yellow jasmine, an apsara

Harimani: emerald

Haripriyā: dear to Vishnu, Lakshmi, earth, basil

Harishree: wonderfully golden, blessed with soma

Haritālikā: goddess of fertility, bringer of greenery

Hareeti: green, verdant, tawny

Harmony: concord

Harnyā: house, mansion, palace

Haroshit: happy, joyful

Harper: harp player, one who plays harp

Harriet: mistress of the home

Harshalā: pleased

Harshaveenā: a lute that delights

Harshi: happy, joyful

Harshini: happy, joy, delight

Harshitā: full of joy

Harshna: happiness

Harshprada: one who gives joy

Harshumati: filled with joy

Hasanti: one who delights, jasmine

Hāsavati: full of laughter

Hasia: protected by god

Hasida: pious

Hasikā: in bloom, smiling, causing laughter

Hasina: good

Hāsini: delightful, an apsara

Hasnā: beautiful

Hasnat: smiling, radiant, blooming

Hasrā: laughing woman, apsara

Hastakamatā: with lotus in hand, Lakshmi

Hasthā: star

Hasumati: always laughing

Hattie: mistress of the home

Havishmati: offering in sacrifices

Hawthorn: from the hawthorn tree

Hayā: modesty

Hayānanā: yogini

Hāyati: flame

Hayi: desire, wish

Haylee: from the hay meadow

Hazel: a tree with nuts, commander

Heather: flower, flowering health

Hedda: refuge in battle

Hedwig: refuge in battle

Hedy: pleasant, sweet

Hedya: voice of the lord

Heerā: diamond, Lakshmi

Heidi: light, dim, noble, nobility, battle maid

Helen: the bright one, light

Helene: light

Helga: holy

Helli: light

Helsa: consecrated to God

Hemā: golden, earth, handsome, a river

Hemabhā: looking like gold

Hemākshi: golden-eyed

Hemalatā: golden vine, yellow jasmine

Hemamālā: golden garland

Hemamālini: garland with gold

Hemangi: golden-bodied

Hemangini: with a golden body

Hemāni: of gold, as precious as gold, Parvati

Hemanti: of winter

Hemapushpikā: with small golden flowers, yellow jasmine

Hemarāgini: coloured gold, turmeric

Hemavamā: golden complexioned

Hemāvati: possessing gold, Parvati, mountain stream

Hemayuthikā: golden, woven, yellow jasmine

Hemamalini: golden creeper

Hemapriya: lover of gold

Hemavathi: name of a river

Hemlatha: golden creeper

Hemshikha: peak of gold

Henriett: home ruler

Henrietta: ruler of home, feminine of Henry

Hephzibah: my joy is in her

Hera: the queen of the gods

Hermione: strong

Hesper: evening star

Hester: star

Hetal: affectionate, happy

Hiba: gift from God

Hibernia: the old latin name for Ireland

Hibiscus: from the flower hibiscus

Hila: praise

Hilary: cheerful

Hilary, Hillary: cheerful, happy

Hilda: battle, maid

Hildegard: battle maid

Hilit: radiance

Himā: snow, night, winter

Hima Bindu: dew drop

Himajā: daughter of snow, Parvati

Himalini: snow-covered

Himāni: snow, glacier, avalanche, Parvati

Himanshi: cool like ice

Himarashmi: white light, cool-rayed, moon, moonlight

Himashailaja: born of snow, Parvati

Himashweta: as white as snow

Himasri: gowri

Himasuta: daughter of snow, fair, calm, Parvati

Himi: snow

Hina: fragrance, myrtle vine

Hinda: deer

Hiran: deer

Hiranya: golden

Hiranyada: giver of gold, earth

Hisa: enduring

Hityashi: well-wisher

Hiya: heart

Hoa: peace

Hollie: holy tree

Holly: plant with red berries

Honey: sweet

Honora: honorable

Hoor: fairy of paradise

Hope: hope

Horacia: feminine of Horace

Hortense: gardener

Hoshi: star

Hotra: invocation

Hridayhari: bewitching

Huberta: feminine of Hubert

Huette: feminine of Hugh

Hulda: an old Testament prophetess, variant of Hilda

Huma: name of the bird phoenix, which regenerates from its own ashes.

Hyacinth: from the flower hyacinth

Hydrangea: from the flower hydrangea

Hyma: goddess Parvati

Hymavathi: goddess Parvati

Hypatia: beautiful and wise 5th century philosopher and mathematician

I

Ianthe: violet flower

Iantha: purple flower

Icelynn: a spree of calm and dazzling personality

Icys: goddess

Iḍā: this moment, intelligence, earth as food-bestower, insight, prosperous

Idalia: behold the sun

Iḍikā: belonging to this moment, earth

Idit: choicest

Iḍiti: one who praises

Iditri: one who appreciates

Idona: industrious

Idonia: love

Ife: love

Ignacia: feminine of Ignace

Ihā: desire, wish, activity, effort

Ihitā: desired

Ihshenyā: deserving to be seen

Ijyā: gift, charity, worship

Ikshā: sight

Ikshitā: seen, visible

Ikshu: sweetness

Ikshudā: giving wishes, bringing joy

Ikshugandhā: fragrant, as sweet smelling as sugarcane

Ikshutā: bringer of sweetness, wish-granting

Ikshulatā: creeper of sweetness

Ikshumati: one who is sweet

Ikshumālini: a sweet person

Ikshumālavi: a person who is sweet

Ikshuvāri: sugarcane juice, the sea of syrup

Ilā: earth, prayers, stream of praise, offering

refreshment, recreation, mother, teacher, priestess, speech

Iladevi: the earth

Ilākshi: eye of the earth, hub of the earth

Ilana: tree

Ilāvilā: having insight, scholar, praise

Ilaka: small form of earth

Ileshā: queen of the earth

Ilhinā: highly intelligent

Ilika: of earth, corporeal

Ilishā: queen of the earth

Ilka: industrious

Ilona: the bright one, light

Ilvikā: protector of the earth

Imān: faith, belief

Imani: faith, trustworthy

Imogene: image

Impanā: sweet-voiced

Ina: a Latin feminine suffix, but in recent times used alone as a name

Inākshi: sharp-eyed

Inari: small or shrimp

Indali: to attain power

Indeevaraprabhā: light of the blue lotus

Indeevarini: collection of blue lotuses

Indirā: bestower of power, bestower of prosperity, Lakshmi

Indrākshi: eyes like Indra

Indraneel: sapphire

Indraneelikā: as blue as Indra

Indrāni: Indra's wife

Indrashakti: energy of Indra

Indratā: the power and majesty of Indra

Indrāyani: wife of Indra

Indu: a bright drop, soma, moon, camphor

Indubhavā: emerging from the moon

Indujā: daughter of the moon, Narmada river

Indukakshā: moon's radiating circle, orbit of the moon

Indukala: a part of the moon

Indukalikā: a small part of the moon

Indukamalā: white lotus

Indukāntā: beloved of the moon, night

Indulekhā: a digit of the moon

Indumathi: wife of king Aja

Indumati: full moon, fair, calm, healing

Induratnā: jewel of the moon, pearl

Induvadanā: with a moon-like face

Inez: pure, chaste, true

Ingrid: daughter

Inikā: earth in a small form

Innogen: girl

Iola: dawn cloud

Iona: purple gem

Ipsā: desire, wish

Ipsitā: desired, wished for

Irā: earth, speech, water, nourishment, refreshment

Irajā: daughter of the wind, primal water

Irāmā: happiness of the earth

Irāvati: clouds, full of milk or water

Irene: peace

Irijayā: victorious wind

Irikā: a small form of earth

Iris: rainbow

Irit: daffodil

Irma: strong

Irvina: feminine of Irving

Isabel: pledged to God, another form of Elizabeth

Isadora: feminine of Isidore

Isar: eminence

Ishā: power, faculty, dominion, Durga

Ishānā: sovereign, Durga

Ishani: possessing, ruling

Ishānikā: belonging to the north-east

Ishikā: painter's brush, pen for auspicious writing

Ishnā: ardent desire

Ishitkā: desired, greatness, superiority

Ishta: that which is worshipped through sacrifice

Ishtara: dearer

Ishttu: desire, wish

Ishuka: arrow, like an arrow, an apsara

Ishwari: goddess

Isis: Egyptian goddess, sister of Osiris

Isla: island, river

Isolda: the fair

Ibhi: an elephant

Ichcha: desire

Idheeka: one who praises

Israela: feminine of Israel

Israt: affectionate

Itara: another

Iti: with me

Itkila: full of fragrance

Ivana: feminine of Ivan

Ivory: faithful, feminine of Ivan, from the white substance of tusks,etc.

Ivy: from the ivy vine, name of an evergreen climbing ornamental plant

Iya: pervading

Iksha: sight

Iti: accomplished, end

Illika: of earth

Ishna: desire

J

Jaanya: life

Jabakusum: flower of meditation, beloved of Krishna

Jabālā: possessor of a herd of goats, a young cowherdess

Jacinta: beautiful

Jacoba: feminine of Jacob

Jacqueline: feminine of Jacques

Jada: wise

Jadambā: mother of the world, Durga

Jade: stone

Jael: she-goat

Jafit: beautiful

Jagadamba: mother of Universe, foddess Parvati

Jagadeeswari: godess Lalithamba

Jagadgauri: fairest of the universe, Parvati

Jagadhātri: universe sustainer, Parvati, Saraswati

Jagajyoti: earth, creator of the world

Jagandāmbikā: with mother of the universe, Durga

Jaganmātā: mother of the world, Durga, Lakshmi

Jaganmohini: Durga

Jagatārini: saviour of the world

Jagatgauri: beauty of the universe

Jagati: of the universe, heaven and hell conjoined, earth

Jagavi: born of the universe

Jāgriti: alert, attentive, not extinguishable, fire, soma

Jāhnavi: earth-born, Ganga

Jaidyn: god has heard

Jaijaiwanti: full of victory, a song of victory

Jailekha: a record of victory, victorious many times

Jaimala: garland of victory

Jaiman: victorious

Jaiprabha: light of victory

Jaipriya: beloved of victory

Jaisheela: character of victory, one who is habitually victorious

Jaisudha: nectar of victory, sweet taste of victory

Jaitvati: bearer of victory, victorious

Jaivanti: long lived, being victorious

Jaivati: winning, being victorious

Jala: full of water, charity

Jalabala: daughter of the water, nymph, Lakshmi

Jalabalika: daughter of the water, lightning as daughter of cloud

Jaladhija: daughter of the ocean, Lakshmi

Jalahasini: smile of water, wife of Krishna

Jalaja: born of the water, Lakshmi

Jalajakshi: lotus-eyed

Jalajata: born of the water, lotus

Jalajini: a group of lotuses

Jalakanta: beloved of water, ocean, wind

Jalakusuma: flower of water, lotus

Jalalata: creeper of water, wave

Jalambika: mother of water, well

Jalandhara: water bearer

Jalaneeli: as blue as water, water nymph

Jalapriya: dear to water, a bird

Jalapushpa: water lily

Jalarnava: ocean of water

Jallata: stream, wave

Jalpa: talk, discussion, discourse

Jama: daughter

Jamarica: America's heart

65

Jambālini: maiden of water

Jameela: beautiful

Jamilā: beautiful

Jamuna: river Yamuna

Jan: feminine of John

Jānā: God's greatest gift, fruit harvest

Janabālikā: very bright, lightning

Janakakumari: king Janak's daughter, Sita

Jānaki: daughter of Janaka

Janani: mother

Janashruti: folklore

Janay: a form of Jane

Janaylin: God has answered with waterfalls

Jane: daughter of God who is perfect, the Lord is gracious, feminine of John

Janelle: a form of Jane

Janeshthā: desired by men, jasmine

Janessa: a form of Jane

Janet: feminine of John

Janhitā: one concerned with people's welfare

Jāni: daughter-in-law, an apsara

Janice: feminine of John

Janie: God is gracious

Janiece: one who walks with the God

Janine: gift from God, variant of John

Janita: a form of Juanita

Janna: God's gracious gift, Swedish feminine form of John

Jannah: heaven, paradise, garden

Jantumati: conceiver, earth

Janujā: born, a daughter

Jari: earthen water jug

Jarita: Sage Mandapala's wife, a bird in Hindu legend who through her devotion to her offspring, became human.

Jārul: queen of flowers, myrtle flower

Jararāni: queen of fame

Jasmine: strong in the heart, beautiful flower, sweet and amiable one

Jasna: clear, bright

Jasrāh: narrator of the Hadith

Jaṭalikā: with twisted hair

Jaṭilā: complex, with twisted hair

Javitri: spice, mace

Jayā: victory, victorious, Parvati

Jayadevi: goddess of victory

Jayalakshmi: goddess of victory

Jayalalitā: as beautiful as victory, the goddess of victory

Jayamālā: garland of victory

Jayanā: bestower of victory

Jayanandini: daughter of victory, daughter of Lakshmi

Jayani: bringer of victory, daughter of Indra

Jayanthi: name of Indras daughter

Jayanti: finally victorious, a flag, daughter of Indra

Jayaprada: one who gives victory

Jayashree: goddess of victory

Jayasri, Jayasree: goddess representing success/victory

Jayde: derivative of Jade, a flirtatious girl; a semiprecious green stone

Jaye: a bird

Jayitā: victorious

Jayitri: victorious

Jayla: a form of Jaye

Jazmyne: tranquility, variation of jasmine

Jeanne: feminine of John

Jeanette: feminine of John

Jeannine: feminine of Gene

Jehān: beautiful flower

Jemimah: dove

Jemina: right-handed

Jemma: dove

Jenn: a short form of Jennifer

Jenna: small bird, heaven, paradise, garden, fair one

Jennah: heaven, paradise, garden, fair one

Jenni: white wave

Jennie: well born

Jennifer: fair lady

Jerusha: inheritance, married or possesed one

Jesamie: short form of Jessica

Jessica: wealthy, God's gift, majesty, virtue

Jessie: wealthy, short form of Jessica

Jetashree: goddess of gains

Jewel: playful, a precious gem

Jhajharika: a goddess

Jhala: girl, heat of the sun

Jambari: enemy of darkness, fire, Indra's thunderbolt, Indra

Jhankana: desire

Jhankarini: producing a tinkling sound, bell, anklet-worn woman, Durga, Ganga

Jharna: flowing down, spring, streamlet, fountain

Jhatalik : lustre, splendour, light

Jhati: shining, glittering, white jasmine

Jhillika: sunshine, light, moth

Jhilmil: sparkling

Jhumari: ornament of the forehead

Jageesha: desire to win

Jill: diminutive of Gillian, youthful

Jillian: girl

Jitavati: best among women, one who has won

Jitya: victorious

Jivanti: flower

Jivantika: bestower of long life

Jivika: source of life, water, occupation

Joan: feminine of John

Joasia: another form of Joanna

Jocelyn: just

Jodie: goddess

Jody: praised

Joella: lord is willing

Joelle: feminine of Joel

Jogū: praising

Jolie: pretty

Jon Benet: little one from God

Jonina: dove

Jordan: to flow down, descend, down-flowing

Jordana: feminine of Jordan

Josephine: feminine of Joseph

Joshā: woman

Joshikā: cluster of buds, young woman

Joshita: delighted

Joshyā: delightful

Josie: dimnutive form of Josephine

Jovanny: father of the land

Joy: joy, delight, happiness

Joyce: just

Juanita: feminine of John, God is gracious

Judith: praised

Judy: praised

Jugishā: one who wishes to be victorious

Jūhi: jasmine

Julaine: form of Julie

Julia: youthful

Julianna: youthful

Julie: feminine form of Julian, young, youthful one

Julius: soft haired, youthful

June: young

Juno: Roman goddess, the wife of Jupiter

Jūrñi: glowing fires, blaze

Justine: feminine of Justin

Jutikā: camphor

Juventina: young Christian

Jwālā: flame, blaze, light, shine

Jwalanā: flaming, shining

Jwālikā: blazing, lighted

Jyotā: the brilliant one

Jyothi: lamp, light

Jyothirmayi: bright girl

Jyothsana: morning sunlight

Jyothsna: moonlight

Jyoti: brilliant, like a flame, dawn, divine light, lightning, fire

Jyotibalā: a domsel flame

Jyositā: a woman

Jyotiskā: giver of light

Jyotsnee: moon-lit night

Jyotika: a small lamp

Jyotinikā: with a shining face

Jyotirlekhā: a line of light

Jyotishmati: luminous, celestial, belonging to the world, brilliant, shining

Jyotsnā: moonlight, night, moonlit night, splendour, Durga

Jyotsni: moonlit night

Janika: producing

Janini: mother

Jalbala: river

Jahnav: Ganga river

Jaiman: victorious

K

Kaali: goddess Durga, blackness, destroyer of time, night, a succession of black clouds

Kaberi: full of water, courtesan

Kabila: beloved

Kadali: banana tree

Kadamba: cloud, group, kadamba tree

Kadambari: emerging from the kadamba tree, female cuckoo, nectar from kadamba, flower, Saraswati

Kadambini: garland of clouds

Kadhapriya: ever loved, ever friendly

Kadia: pitcher

Kadru: tawny, soma vessel, earth in a personified form

Kahala: mischievous, young woman, an apsara

Kahini: mischievous, young

Kaihla: version of kayla

Kaila: laurel, crown

Kailee: form of Kaila

Kaileshwari: goddess of water, Durga

Kairavi: moonlight

Kairavini: water-born, white lotus plant

Kaitlan: pure

Kaitlynn: an alternate form of Caitlyn, pure

Kajal: collyrium, kohl

Kajri: collyrium-coloured, like a cloud

Kakali: cuckoo-voiced, a musical instrument

Kakalika: with a sweet and low voice

Kakini: a small coin

Kakshi: of jungle, fragrant earth, perfume

Kakubha: peak, splendour, beauty, wealth of flowers

Kakud: peak, symbol of royalty

Kakul: fleaks of hair

Kala: art, a small point, a part of the moon, an atom, still

Kalai: art

Kalaiselvi: art, wealthy girl, artist

Kalakanya: daughter of tune

Kalandika: bestower of art and skills, wisdom, intelligence

Kalanisha: night of Diwali

Kalanit: anemone

Kalapini: as blue as peacock's tail, night

Kalavati: moonlight, well-versed in arts

Kalavinka: cuckoo

Kaleshika: black sandalwood

Kalee: destroyer of time, night

Kali: bud

Kalib: of God

Kalidasa: servant of Goddess Kali

Kalifa: holy

Kalika: dark blue, black, fragrant earth, fog, Durga

Kalika: bid, tender, fragrant, progressive

Kalila: beloved

Kalindi: river Yamuna

Kallolini: ever happy, surging stream

Kalmia: mountain laurel

Kalob: of God

Kalpalata: wish-giving creeper

Kalpana: imagination, decoration

Kalpataru: wish-granting tree

Kalpavati: virtuous

Kalya: eulogy, praise

Kalyanavati: propitious, beneficial, fortunate, excellent, Parvati

Kalyani: auspicious, happy, beautiful

Kama: beauty, radiance

Kamada: granting wishes

Kamaduha: granter of desires

Kamadyu: granter of wishes

Kāmādhyā: granter of wishes, Durga

Kāmākshī: with beautiful and large eyes, Durga

Kamal: born of a lotus, beautiful, wealth, spring, desirous, Lakshmi

Kamala: lotus, goddess Lakshmi

Kamalanayani: lotus-eyed

Kamaleekā: a small lotus

Kamalekshanā: lotus-eyed

Kamali: collection of lotuses, water, crane

Kamalini: lotus plant, collection of lotuses, fragrant, auspicious, beautiful, dear to the Gods

Kāmanā: desire

Kamania: like the moon

Kāmāyakā: desired abode

Kāmāyani: mirror of love

Kambria: Latin name for wales

Kameelah: perfect

Kāmikā: desired

Kamila: perfect one

Kāmini: desirable, loving, beautiful

Kāmitā: wished for, desired

Kamiya: wish

Kāmrā: lovable, wish, desire

Kāmodi: that which excites

Kamrā: beautiful, attractive, loving

Kāmuka: desired

Kāmyā: desirable, beautiful, amiable

Kanā: girl, eye

Kanak: corn

Kanaka: gold

Kānakā: born of sand, Sita

Kanakalatā: golden vine

Kanakāmbarā: dressed in gold, golden, a flower

Kanakambari: woman wearing gold ornaments, name of a flower

Kanakaprabhā: gold-lustred, golden bright

Kanakāvati: golden chain

Kanakavallī: golden creeper

Kanakavati: possessor of gold, golden

Kanakvi: a small kite

Kānan: forest, grove

Kānanalatā: forest maiden

Kanchamala: gold necklace

Kanchan: gold

Kanchana: gold necklace

Kanchanā: that which shines, wealth

Kānchanamālā: garland of gold

Kānchanaprabhā: as bright as gold

Kānchapi: connoisseur of glory, Saraswati's lute

Kānchi: shining, belled waistband

Kandarā: lute, hollow, cave

Kandharā: water bearer, cloud

Kandicec: nice and wealthy, glowing

Kanganā: bracelet

Kaneech: creeper with blossoms

Kaneenā: youthful, pupil of the eye, little finger

Kani: girl

Kanikā: small, diminutive, girl

Kanishthā: little finger, youngest

Kanitā: iris of the eye

Kanjari: bird, a musical instrument

Kankā: perfume of the lotus

Kananā: bracelet, ornament, crest

Kankanika: small bell, tinkling ornament

Kanksha: desire, inclination

Kankshini: one who desires

Kannaki: devoted wife

Kannikā: maiden

Kāntā: beloved, perfume, earth

Kanteli: irresistible

Kanthi: light, radiance, glow

Kānti: beauty, glory, wish, decoration, a part of the moon

Kanyā: daughter, maiden

Kanyakā: maiden, the smallest, daughter

Kanyakaparameswari: name of a goddess

Kanyalā: girl

Kanyanā: maiden

Kanyāratnā: a gem of a girl

Kapālikā: Kali

Kapālini: Durga

Kapardikā: a small shell

Kapilā: daughter of Daksha

Kapishā: a river

Kara: pure

Karam: generosity

Karavini: strong-armed, oleander flower

Karen: pure

Kari: strong, feminine, pure

Karishmā: miracle

Karishni: goddess of wealth

Karkari: lute

Karidā: untouched, virginal

Karin: variant form of Katherine, pure

Karina: dear little one, variant of Katherine, pure

Karishma: miracle

Karisma: miracle

Karma: destiny

Karmishthā: very diligent

Karni: a good listener

Karnikā: creeper, heart of a lotus, earring

Karol: feminine form of Carl

Karole: joyous song

Karoli: Parvati

Kārpani: gladness

Karpūri: camphor-scented

Kārtiki: full-moon night, pious, holy

Karuṇā: compassion, tenderness

Karunesh: goddess

Karuṇyā: compassionate, praiseworthy, merciful

Kasen: pure

Kasey: clever, alert, vigorous

Kasha: beautiful

Kāshi: splendid, shining, sun

Kashish: an attraction towards

Kashmirā: a tree

Kāshvi: beautiful, shining

Kassandra: unheeded prophetess

Kastūri: musk-scented

Kasturikā: musk

Kate: pure

Katelyne: beloved, pure

Katharina: pure, virgin

Katherine: pure

Kathleen: little darling

Kathrina: pure

Kathy: diminutive, Katherine

Katiana: princess

Katie: the most popular English short form of Katherine

Katrien: variant of Catherine

Katrina: one of purity, beloved

Kātyāyani: clad in red, Parvati

Kaukulikā: belonging to the universe

Kaumāri: virgin, Parvati

Kaushalikā: present, offering

Kausalyā: welfare, cleverness, skill

Kaushikā: drinking vessel, silk, cup

Kaushiki: covered, silken, Durga

Kautukā: giving pleasure, causing admiration, arousing curiosity

Kāvali: bangle

Kāveri: full of water, courtesan, turmeric

Kavikā: poetess

Kavitā: poem

Kavya: literary composition, poem

Kay: pure, keeper of the keys

Kaycee: alert, vigorous

Kayeigh: a happy gathering

Kayla: laurel, crown, pure, slim & fair

Kaylah: of God

Kaylay: variant of Kay (pure, keeper of the keys)

Kaylee: laurel, crown

Kayleigh: variant of Kay (pure, keeper of the keys)

Kaylie: feminine form of Kyle

Kedma: towards the east

Keeley: brave warrior, beautiful, pretty

Keeli: parrot

Keelie: variant of Kelly

Keelin: slender, fair

Keely: graceful

Keerthi: fame

Keerti: glory, fame, renown

Keertidā: bestower of fame

Keertimālini: garlanded with fame

Keiko: beloved

Keisha: short form of Keneisha

Kelakā: sportive, one who knows the arts, artiste, playful

Kelda: a spring

Kelila: crown of laurel

Kellee: lively, aggressive

Kelli: lively, aggressive

Kelly: lively, aggressive, warrior, brave

Kelsey: the ships from the vikings, dweller by the sea, brave

Kelsy: fountain, spring

Kelsie: ship island, seaport

Ken: one's own kind

Kenāti: exceling all

Kendra: knowing woman, wisdom, centre

Keneisha: Ken and Aisha

Kenya: animal horn, a country in Africa

Keosha: lovely, one that posses beauty

Kerrie: powerful female ruler, great dark one

Kerrilynn: dusky, dark, dark one

Kerrin: animal's horn

Kerry: dark one

Kesari: scented like saffron

Keshayantri: long-haired

Keshika: long-haired

Keshini: long-haired, Durga

Kesley: bitter, graceful

Ketaki: golden, a flower

Ketimati: gifted with brightness

Keturah: incense

Ketzia: fragrant

Kevika: a flower

Kezia: variant of Kesia, short form of Lakeisha, favorite

Khadijah: premature born

Khala: mischievous

Khalida: immortal

Khandini: made of parts, earth

Kharika: powered musk

Kharjuri: reaching the skies, date tree

Khaseeraja: milk

Khasha: perfume, pervading the air

Kheli: moving in the sky, sun, bird, hymn, arrow

Khimya: mercy

Khushi: happiness

Khyati: perception, celebrity, hymn of praise, idea, knowledge, glory, view, Lakshmi

Kiara: to make a change

Kiera: beautiful little dark haired one

Kierra: beautiful

Kiki: bhuejay (bird)

Kim: from the meadow of the royal fortress

Kimala: butterfly

Kimberly: chief, ruler

Kimnari: singer

Kimpuna: small and pious

Kimshuka: a tiny parrot

Kinjatā: brook

Kinkanā: small bell

Kinnari: a Lady who sings with beautiful voice

Kinneret: harp

Kiran: light, ray

Kiranmayi: one glowing with radiance, bright girl, intelligent girl

Kirmi: an image of gold

Kirsten: the Anointed one, feminine of Christian.

Kirsṭen: stone church

Kirstin: feminine of Christian

Kishori: maiden, adolescent

Kitāl: nectar, wine

Kitiana: clear eyes

Kohā: cuckoo, date tree, Vishnu

Kohavah: star

Kohinoor: mountain of light

Kokila: Indian cuckoo

Kolambi: Shiva's lute

Komalā: soft, tender, delicate, beautiful

Korrin: maiden

Koshin: bud, mango, Durga

Kousalya: Sri Rama's mother, king Dasharatha's wife

Koyal: Indian cuckoo

Kranti: revolutionary

Kraunchi: heron, snipe (bird)

Krinjalā: brook

Kripā: compassion, kindness, favour

Krishnā: night, dark, pupil of the eye, a plant with dark blossoms, perfume, Durga

Krishna Kumari: daughter of Krishna

Krishnāngi: black-bodied, parrot

Krishna Priya: beloved of Lord Krishna

Krishnavalli: dark-leaved, basil

Krishna Veni: one with dark hair

Krishni: dark night

Krissa: variant form of Christine

Krista: follower of Christ

Kristin: Christian

Kristine: Christ bearer, variant of Christine

Kriti: creation, action

Krittika: name of a star

Kriyā: action, performance, work

Kritadyuti: with accomplished glory

Kritamālā: garland maker

Kritee: creation, accomplishment, enchantment

Krittikā: star-covered

Kritvi: accomplished

Krityā: replete with achievements, right, magical rites, proper

Krityahā: full of achievements

Krysia: little Christine, derived from Christine

Kshamā: mercy, patience, of earth, the number one, Durga

Kshamāvati: with a merciful mind

Kshamāvati: one who is compassionate, enduring, forbearing

Kshamyā: earth

Kshavyā: of the earth

Kshanadā: bestower of moment or leisure, bestower of life, water, night

Kshānti: patience, endurance, indulgence

Kshapā: night

Kshatriyāni: wife of a noble warrior

Kshemā: welfare, security, tranquillity, bliss

Kshemagiri: mountain of security, full of security

Kshemakari: bestowing happiness and peace and security, Durga

Kshemyā: goddess of wealth, Durga

Kshiprā: fast

Kshirasāgarā: sea of milk

Kshirin: milky

Kshiti: abode, habitation, earth, soil of the earth, settlements, races of men

Kshitijā: born of the earth, Sita

Kshonā: immovable, earth

Kuhārita: song of the cuckoo

Kuhū: cry of the cuckoo

Kujā: daughter of the earth, horizon, Sita, Durga

Kulāngana: highborn woman

Kulyā: virtuous, well born

Kumālikā: cuckoo

Kumani: maiden, daughter, gold, jasmine, Durga, Sita

Kumarādevi: goddess of children

Kumārikā: girl, virgin, jasmine, Durga, Sita

Kumbhikā: a small water jar

Kumbhini: jar-shaped, earth

Kumkum: red, saffron, pollen

Kumud: lily, red, lotus

Kumudākshā: lotus-eyed, red-eyed

Kumudikā: bearer or wearer of water lilies

Kumudini: collection of white lilies

Kundā: flower

Kundanikā: jasmine

Kundini: collection of jasmines

Kunjika: belonging to the flower, nutmeg flower

Kunshi: shining

Kuntal: hair

Kuntalā: perfume, lock of hair, plough

Kunti: mother of Pandavas and Karna, Kunti Devi

Kuralayita: adorned with water lilies

Kurangākshi: beautiful, doe-eyed

Kurangi: deer, spot in the moon

Kureerā: head ornament

Kuri: chestnut

Kushbu: fragrance

Kusuma: flower

Kusumā: like a flower, a blossom, yellow champaka flower

Kusuma Latha: flowering creeper

Karikā: actress

Katikee: holy, Kartik's full moon

Kāshtā: direction

Kāsu: luster

Kusumānjali: offering of flowers

Kusumitā: adorned with flower

Kuvalayini: abounding in water lilies

Kuvira: warrior

Kyla: feminine of Kyle

Kylara: bay

Kylee: from the straight

Kylie: boomerang

Kāver: safron

Kritvee: accomplished

Kshunu: five

Kumuda: a red lotus flower, white water lily

Kshiti: the earth

L

Lābuki: lute

Lacey: cheerful

Lael: devoted to the Lord

Laghupushpā: delicate flower

Lahari: wave

Laila: sweet heart

Lainey: sun ray

Lajja: modesty

Lajjana: modest

Lajjita: sky, coy, modest

Lajwanti: sensitive plant

Lajya: modesty

Lakia: found treasure

Lākini: one who takes and gives

Laksha: lac, plant

Lākshaki: dyed with lac, relating to lac

Lakshi: Lakshmi

Lakshitā: beheld, distinguished

Lakshmi: fortune, prosperity, splendour, beauty, charm, success, pearl, goddess of fortune, turmeric

Lala: tulip

Lalana: a girl

Lalantikā: a long necklace

Lalatikā: forehead ornament

Lālima: reddish glow, beautiful, charming, forehead ornament, symbol, banner

Lalitā: woman, desirable, lovely, Durga, soft, gentle, graceful, voluptuous

Lalitha: goddess Parvati, beauty

Lalitaka: favourite daughter

Lalitāngi: with a beautiful body

Lalitasyā: grace, charm, beauty

Lālli: radiance, sweatness, blush, prestige

Lāluka: necklace

Lambadi: name of a tribe

Lambushā: a dangling ornament

Lamita: beautiful, charming eyes

Lana: bouyant, float, to bring, light and buoyant, an offering, dear child

Langapriyā: adorable

Lani: heavenly

Lapitā: spoken, speech, voice

Lara: renowned, protection

Laramie: tears of love

Larina: seagull

Larissa: cheerful,

Larretta: diminuitive/ alternate form of Laura

Larrna: joy

Lasa Priya: Lakshmi

Lashā: saffron, turmeric

Latā: vine, slender woman, a string of pearls

Laṭabhā: beautiful, handsome

Latāmaṅi: coral

Latha: creeper plant

Lathangi: girl with creeper like slim body

Latikā: forehead ornament, string of pearls, a small creeper

Latona: Roman name for the Greek Goddess Leto, mother of Apollo and Diana

Laura: victoriously crowned with laurels, feminine of Lawrenece

Laurel: the laurel tree, sweet bay tree, symbolic of honour and victory, victorious

Lauren: feminine of Lawrenece

Lauretta: diminutive/ alternate form of Laura

Lavalee: vine, custard apple

Lavaleekā: tiny vine

Lavaleenā: devoted, enraptured

Lavaṅā: lustrous, beautiful

Lavaneetā: extremely beautiful

Lavangi: of the clove plant

Lāvanyā: extremely beautiful

Lavanya: grace, beauty, beautiful lady

Lavañyamayi: full of beauty, full of charm

Lavender: precious site

Lavenia: purified; woman of Rome

Laverne: spring like

Lavinia: woman of Rome

Layla: born at night

Layne: little one from the lane

Laynee: God's blessings poured out

Lea: the goddess of canoe makers, fatigued beauty

Leah: the weary one, the weak-sighted one, wild cow, gazelle

Leahcar: goddess of party

Leandra: feminine of Leander

Leanne: combination of Lee and Anne

Leatrice: combination of Lee and Beatrice

Leda: mythological wife of Zeus, and mother of Helen and of Castor and Pollux

Lee: glade, poet, plum

Leela: play, amusement, beauty, grace, pleasure, ease

Leelavati: playful, beautiful, graceful, charming, Durga

Leena: absorbed, merged, engrossed

Leigh: meadow

Leila: dark as night

Leilani: heavenly flower, heavenly child

Leisje: consecrated to God

Lekha: line, streak, lightning, figure, mark, crescent moon, horizon, crest

Lekisha: life, a combination of prefix La and Keisha

Lemuela: feminine of Lemuel

Lena: pearl

Lenore: pledge

Leona: feminine of Leo

Leonarda: feminine of Leonard

Leonora: light

Leontine: feminine of Leo

Leopolda: feminine of Leopold

Leora: my light

Lepākshi: with painted eyes

Leslie: dweller in grey castle

Leslyan: caring one

Letitia: joy

Levana: the moon

Levona: spice

Lexus: defender of man kind

Lezhai: dragon dance

Lian: my joy

Liānā: creeper plant

Liat: you are mine

Libby: consecrated to God

Libra: balance

Libujā: vine

Liesbet: God is bountiful

Liesbeth: God is bountiful, variant of Elisabeth

Lilac: from the flower lilac

Lilian: lily like tender and beautiful girl

Lilith: of the night

Lill: flower

Lillian: lily

Lily: name of a flower, pure, innocent and beautiful like a lily flower

Limor: myrrh

Lina: palm tree (Arabic meaning)

Linda: pretty one

Linden: the linden tree

Lindi: pretty

Lindsay: port, island

Lindsey: trees near the water, pool on an island

Line: distinguished one

Linnet: bird

Linette: from the linnet, a song bird

Lipikā: alphabet, writing, anointing, manuscript

Liraz: my secret

Lisa: dedicated to God, short form of Elisabeth

Livia: feminine of Oliver

Liza: short form of Elizabeth

Lleyke: light

Lochanā: eye, brightening, illuminating

Lohamukhitā: red pearl

Lohitā: red, ruby

Lohitākshi: red-eyed

Lohitamukti: ruby

Lohitāyani: red

Lohitikā: ruby

Lohityā: rice

Lois: feminine of Louis

Lokavyā: a deserver of heaven

Loksakshini: beholder of universe, goddess

Lolā: Lakshmi

Lolikā: a kind of sorrel

Lolini: woman

Lolita: from the Virgin Mary

Lolitā: sorrows

Londyn: fortress of the Moon

Lonikā: beautiful woman

Lonna: solitary

Lorelai: victorious spirit

Lorelei: ruler to the rocks

Lorenza: crowned with laurel

Loretah: diminutive/alternate form of Laura

Loretta: pure

Lorette: diminutive/alternate form of Laura

Lorietta: diminutive/alternate form of Laura

Lorita: diminutive/alternate form of Laura

Lorna: forsaken

Lorraine: from the medieval kingdom of Lorraine

Lotikā: light reddish-brown

Lotta: feminine of Charles

Lottie: feminine of Charles

Lotus: from the lotus flower

Louella: feminine of Louis

Lousia: feminine of Louis

Lovia: loveable lady, beautiful, graceful.

Lovina: love, kindness, charity

Loyanā: eye

Luba: lover

Lucerne: life

Lucianna: feminine of Lucian

Lucille: light

Lucky: favoured by fortune

Lucretia: gain, reward

Lucy: light, illumination

Ludmilla: loved by the people

Luellā: elfin

Lulu: light, precious

Luna: moon

Luni: Ganga

Lupitā: Sage Mandapala's wife

Lumbikā: a kind of musical instrument

Lapitā: spoken

Libnee: a manuscript of God

Luwanna: pretty girl

Luz: almond tree

Luzetta: light

Lydia: woman of Lydia

Lyndy: pretty

Lyndsey: from linden tree

Lynelle: pretty

Lynette: flowing brook

Lynn: cascade

Lyra: of the lyre, the words of a song

Lyric: of the lyre, the words of a song

Lyrica: of the lyre, the words of a song

Lyris: of the harp or lyre

Lyudmyla: people like her

Lopā: loss

Lohitiyā: rice

Laugheyee: copper coloured

M

Maanami: beautiful

Maanasa: name of a lake in the Himalayas, birth place of river Ganga

Mabel: lovable

Machiko: beautiful child, child that learns truth

Mackenna: form of Mackenzie

Mackenzie: daughter of the wise leader

Madanlekhā: love letter, love sequence

Madanamanchūkā: aroused

Madanamajari: bird of love

Madani: vine, musk

Madanikā: excited, aroused

Madanayanti: exciting, jasmine, Durga

Madanyantikā: exciting, jasmine

Madayati: exciting, jasmine

Madeline: woman from Magdala

Mādhavā: exotic, full of intoxication, exciting

Madhavashree: vernal beauty

Mādhavi: sweet, date flower, basil, intoxicating drink, Durga

Mādhavikā: collector of honey, creeper

Madhu: sweet, honey, soma, nectar, water

Madhubālā: sweet maiden

Madhudhārā: stream of honey

Madhudivā: excited by honey, excited by spring, intoxicated

Madhujā: made of honey, honeycomb, earth

Madhukakshā: sweetness, dew

Madhūlikā: sweetness, bee, mustard

Madhumādhavi: a spring flower full of honey

Madhumathi: girl with sweet nature, Lakshmi

Madhumati: rich in honey, spring-intoxicated, sweet, pleasant, agreeable

Madhumeeta: sweet friend

Madhumita: very sweet

Madhupratika: sweet-mouthed, with qualities of a yogini

Madhupushpa: spring flower, rain

Madhurakshi: with beautiful eyes

Madhuri: sweetness, charm, wine, syrup, jasmine, a musical instrument

Madhurima: sweetness, loveliness, charm

Madhurya: sweetness, tender affection, charm, exquisite beauty

Madhushi: bountiful, generous

Madhushree: beauty of spring

Madhuvalini: gifted with nectar

Madhuwati: with a heady beauty

Madhuvidya: sweet knowledge

Madhwija: born of honey, an intoxicating drink

Madira: nectar, wine, intoxicating liquor

Madiravati: with intoxicating beauty

Madirekshana: with intoxicating eyes

Madison: good

Madonna: my lady

Mae: great

Maggie: short form of Margaret

Magha: gift, wealth, reward

Maghee: giving presents

Maghya: jasmine blossom

Maha: great, cow

Mahadyota: extremely shining

Mahajava: extremely fleet-footed

Mahajaya: extremely victorious

Mahalakshi: of the great sky

R

Rabi: light

Rachana: arrangement

Rachel: ewe, female sheep

Rachnā: creation, accomplishment, production

Raḍellā: elfin, advisor

Rādhā: full-moon day, lightning, prosperity, success

Rādhanā: speech

Rādhani: worship

Radhikā: prosperous, successful, Radha

Rae: doe

Rafaela: healer from God

Rāgā: beauty, melody, feeling, harmony, passionate

Rāgalatā: passion creeper

Rāgamayā: full of passion, red, full of colour, full of love, dear, beloved

Rāgavati: full of love, beloved, coloured

Rāgiñi: melody, love, attachment, Lakshmi

Rahni: love, affection

Rāhuratnā: jewel of Rahu, hyacinth

Rainā: night

Rajalakshmi: royal dignity

Rajarajeswari: godess Lalithamba

Rāji: night

Rajini: night

Rajyavati: princess, possessing a kingdom

Rākānishā: full-moon night

Rāki ñi: night

Rakshā: protection, a charm or amulet for protection

Rakshāmani: jewel of protection

Rakshanā: protecting, safeguarding

Rakshi: wife of Sun god, queen

Rakshitā: protected

Raktā: red, painted, beloved, pleasant, dear

Raktahansā: red swan, happy soul

Raktakanchan: red gold

Raktakumud: red lotus

Raktapadmā: red lotus

Raktapallavā: red leaf, with red leaves

Raktapushpā: red-flowered, pomegranate blossom

Ramā: beautiful, charming, enchanting, fortune, opulence, red earth, splendour, vermilion

Ramādevi: goddess of beauty, lovely woman

Rāmakeli: sport of Lakshmi

Rāmakiri: of omnipresent nature, all-pervading

Ramakrit: causing rest

Rāmala: lover, bestower of pleasure

Ramana: enchanting, worthy of being loved, beloved, charming

Ramanaa: a charming woman, a wife

Ramaneetā: elegance, beauty

Ramani: beautiful, charming, delighting, joy, loving, pleasure, sexual union

Ramanikā: worth loving, attractive, pleasing

Ramatārā: star of fortune, basil plant

Rāmāyani: mirror of Rama, one well versed in the *Ramayana*

Rambhā: agreeable, lovable, pleasing, staff, plantain

Ramila: with heart and soul

Rāmitā: bestower of pleasure, lover

Ramyā: enchanting, enjoyable

Ramyarūpā: with a lovely form

Ramyashree: most desired

Ranadā: making a sound, bestower of battles

Ranhita: efficient, quick

Ranjita: victorious in battle

Ranlakshmi: goddess of war, fortunes of war

Rangabhūti: born of love, full-moon night

Rangaja: born of love, vermilion

Rangamāñikyā: beloved to Krishna

Rangati: coloured, agreeable, excited, lovable, passionate

Rangita: charmed, coloured, delighted, painted

Ranhita: quick, swift

Rani: queen

Ranjana: charming, exciting, pleasing, perfume, saffron, turmeric

Ranjika: pleaser, charming, pleasing, exciting, love, red sandalwood

Ranjini: amusing, charming, colouring, delighting, entertaining, pleasing

Ranjita: coloured, delighted, made happy, pleased

Rāno: peacock's tail

Ranvā: agreeable, delightful, gay, joyous, pleasant

Ranvita: gay, joyous

Ranya: pleasant

Rasā: essence, grapes, juice, love, charm, delight, nectar, passion, quicksilver, sentiment

Rāsā: full of essence, full of sentiments, play, noise, sport

Rasana: knower of taste, taste, perception

Rasanika: full of feeling, impassioned

Rasapriya: fond of juice

Rasavanti: charming, delighting, emotional, sentimental

Rashana: cord, rope, ray of light, perfume

Rashika: elegant, full of passion, aesthetic, with discrimination, tasteful, sentimental

125

Rashmi: sunbeam, moonbeam, ray, rope

Rashmika: tiny ray of light

Rasika: aesthetic, elegant, gracious

Rasila: interesting person

Raswanti: affection

Rasya: with essence, emotional, full of feelings, juicy, sentimental

Rathachitra: like a multicoloured chariot

Rathantara: one who sits inside the chariot

Rathantari: dweller of the chariot

Rathya: crossword, highway, group of chariots

Rati: love, desire, pleasure, passion, enjoyment, part of the moon

Rathihara: causing pleasure

Ratija: daughter of truth

Ratimada: intoxicated with love

Ratipreeti: love, pleasure, passion, conjoined

Ratna: jewel

Ratnakala: piece of jewel

Ratnamala: jewelled necklace

Ratnamalavati: with a necklace of jewels

Ratnamanjari: jewel, blossom

Ratnambari: clad in jewels

Ratnangi: with jewelled limbs

Ratnaprabha: the shine of jewels, earth

Ratnarashi: collection of jewels, sea

Ratnarekha: line of jewels, ornamented, very precious, very gracious, embellished

Ratnasu: producing jewels, earth

Ratnavali: necklace of jewels

Ratnavar: best among precious things, gold

Ratnavati: full of jewels, earth

Ratnolka: jewelled meteor

Ratnottama: best jewel

Ratri: might

Ratridevi: goddess of the night, white lotus opening at night, moon

Ratrika: night

Ratu: truthful, true, speech, Ganga

Ratiya: daughter of truth

Raupya: silvery, made of silver

Raveena: sun

Raven: black bird

Ravichandrika: glory of sun, moonlight

Ravija: born of the sun

Ravipriya: beloved of the sun

Ravishta: beloved of the sun, orange tree

Rayna: peaceful, queen, alternate form of Reina

Raynae: counsel

Rea: doe, short form of Rachel, flower name for Poppy

Reanna: variant of Rhiannon

Reba: short form of Rebecca

Rebecca: tied, knotted, one who brings peace

Rebha: singer of praise

Rediata: goddess

Reem: gazelle, deer, seed, goddess Durga

Reena: rhythm, dissolved, melted

Reena: melted, dissolved

Reeti: auspiciousness, course, motion, prosperity, remembrance, protection, streak, stream

Reetika: of stream, brass

Regan: reigning, kingly

Regina: queen

Reiko: pretty, lovely child

Reina: queen

Rejakshi: fiery eyes

Rekha: line, streak

Rena: peace, short form of Irene and Irena

Renata: reborn

Renea: beautiful, reborn

Renee: reborn, short form of Irene

Renu: earth, atom, molecule, particle

Renuka: name of sage Jamadagni's wife

Reñukā: born of dust

Re ñumati: pollen-laden

Reshmā: silken

Reshman: silky, soothing

Reshmi: smooth, silky

Revā: mover, agile, quick, swift

Revathi: name of a star, name of Balarama's wife

Revati: wealth, prosperity

Reza: pleasure

Rhea: flowing stream

Rheanna: graceful, stream of grace mercy and prayers

Rhiannon: maiden

Rhoda: rose

Rhonda: fierce waters

Rhonḍā: good spear

Ria: river

Riah: river

Rianna: hope

Ribhyā: worshipped

Richā: praise, hymn, splendour, collection of *Vedas*

Richelle: powerful ruler, brave one

Riddhi: abundance, prosperity, success, wealth, supremacy, supernatural power, Lakshmi, Parvati

Riddhimā: prosperous, successful

Ridū: charming, pleasant, soft

Riham: steady rain

Rihānā: sweet basil

Rijuvani: giving liberally, earth

Rikshā: the best, star, female bear

Rikshambika: mother of the stars, mother of bears

Riley: courageous and valiant

Rima: love

Rinki: regal one

Risa: sunshine, laughter, happiness

Rishikā: female sage

Rishṭā: sword, mother of apsaras

Rita: honest

Rita: season

Ritika: flowing stream

Ritu: season

Ritu Pande: season of learnedness

Riya: singer

Roberta: bright, famous

Robin: famous

Rochamana:consisting of light, agreeable, bright, shining, splendid

Rochelle: large stone, alternate form of Rachel

Rochna: brightness, light, beautiful, handsome, woman, bright sky, red, lotus

Rochani: delightful, agreeable

Rochi: beam, light, ray

Rochiras: aura, glow, light

Rochuka: causing pleasure, pleaser, delighter

Rodasi: heaven and earth conjoined, earth

Rohanti: climbing, vine

Rohee: rising up, red, doe

Rohini: name of a star

Rohini: ascending, increasing, tall, mother of cows, red cow, sandalwood tree

Rohita: red, daughter of Brahma

Roma: full of hair

Romasha: with thick hair

Romola: charming, thick-haired

Roopa: shape, form, figure, beauty, mark

Roopali: pretty, made of silver

Roopini: one with beautiful appearance

Ropana: causing to grow, healing

Rori: famous ruler

Rosa: rose

Rosalie: fair rose

Rosalinda: beautiful rose

Rosetta: a rose

Roshansa: desire, wish

Roshini: eyesight, light

Rosio: drops of dew

Rosita: little rose

Rouha: soul, spirit

Rowenā: red-haired, rugged

Roxane: sunrise, dawn, first light of the day

Royimā: ascending, growing

Rishmā: moonbeam

Rishvā: high, great, noble, elevated

Ritu: fixed time, period, season, order

Ritumbharā: of divine truth, filled with season, earth

Ritushree: queen of the seasons, splendour of the seasons

Ritusthalā: abode of light, abode of seasons

Ruby: precious stone

Ruchā: brightness, desire, light, splendour, voice of the mynah

Ruchi: taste, beauty, desire, light, lustre, pleasure

Ruchikā: of taste, desirable, shining, ornament

Ruchirā: charming, dainty, desirable, pleasing, dainty

Ruchitā: sweet, bright, dainty, desirable, radiant, pleasing, lover

Rūdhi: birth, ascent, fame, rise

Rudrāni: Parvati

Rudrapushpa: red blossom, China rose

Rudrasi: red, like Rudra

Rudy: famous wolf

Ruhā: risen, mounted, grown

Ruhāni: spiritual, of higher values

Rūhi: ascending, of higher value, soul

Ruhikā: riser, longing, desire

Rukma: gold

Rukmarekhā: golden line

Rukmavati: possessing gold, as beautiful as gold, golden

Rukmini: mother of Pradyumna, an incarnation of Lakshmi, queen of Krishna

Rumā: salty, salt mine, ornament

Rumaisa: white as milk

Rumana: pomegranate, heavenly fruit

Rumnita: beautiful

Rūpā: bearer of former silver, earth

Rupal: beautiful, handsome

Rūpāli: beautiful, excellent in form

Rūpāngi: with a beautiful body

Rūpashree: divinely beautiful

Rūpasi: beautiful

Rupasri: divinely beautiful

Rūplekhā: appearance

Rūpmani: beautiful maiden

Rūpmati: possessing beauty

Rūpshikā: crest of beauty, very beautiful

Rūpvati: possessed with beauty, handsome

Rūpavidyā: form of knowledge

Rūpeshwari: goddess of beauty

Rūpikā: having a form and figure, shape, appearance, gold coin, silver coin

Rūpinikā: having a beautiful form, corporeal, embodied

Rupwanti: beautiful girl

Rushmā: calm, angerless

Rūsanā: adorning, covering, decoration

Rushati: white, fair in complexion

Ruth: angelic form

Rutika: ascender, wish

Ryaan: little ruler

S

Sabelle: short form of Isabel, Elizabeth, dedicated to God

Sabina: one with beautiful eyes

Sabine: sublime woman

Sabira: patient

Sabita: politeness, decency, civilised, good manners

Sable: black

Sabra: to rest

Sabra: princess in the woods, thorny

Sabrina: a goddess

Sacheeta: attentive, thoughtful

Sachi, Sachi Devi: name of Indra's wife, fortunate, benediction

Sachu: happiness, pleasure

Sadajyoti: eternal lamp

Sadakanta: always loved

Sadasheesh: good blessing

Sadashiva: ever belonging to Shiva, ever kind and happy, Durga

Sade: short form of Folasade, an African name meaning honour confers a crown

Sadhaka: efficient, effective, magical, productive, Durga

Sadhana: achievement, fulfilment

Sadhana: accomplishment, adorations, means, performance, worship

Sadhika: accomplished, efficient, skilful, worshipper, Durga

Sadhri: conqueror

Sadhunisha: very calm night

Sadhvi: chaste, faithful, honest, noble, pious, peaceful, virtuous, unerring

Sadhya: perfection, accomplishment

Sadie: princess

Sadira: lotus

Sadvati: pious, righteous, truthful

Safa: clarity, purity of mind

Saffron: from a crocus (flower), expensive and rare

Safiyah: pure, friend

Sagarakakshi: living in the ocean's whirlpool

Sagarambara: ocean-clad, earth

Sagarnemi: enriched by the ocean, earth

Sagari: of the ocean

Sage: wise one

Sahadevi: mighty goddess, protected by the goddesses

Sahaja: natural

Sahajanya: produced together

Sahana: tolerant, patient

Sahara: wilderness, name of a desert

Sahara: solace

Saheli: friend, attached with, small minaret

Sahima: with snow

Sahita: being near

Sahitra: full of patience, enduring

Sahuri: full of heat, victorious, mighty, strong, earth

Saida: zaida, huntress, fortunate

Saida: fortunate

Sailaja: godess Parvati

Sailuksha: goddess

Sairandhri: maid

Sajani: sweetheart, worthy companion

Sajeela: decoration

Sajitha: derived from Sajja

Sajja: covered, dressed, ornamented, armed, fortified

Sakalasiddhi: possessing all perfection

Sakhi: generous, bountiful

Sakina: peace of mind, tranquillity

Sākri: of Indra, wife of Indra

Saksham: capable of doing things

Sākshi: witness, with eyes

Sakuchanā: abashed

Salatā: soma, juice-yielding plant

Saleema: simple

Salena: the moon

Sālikā: flute

Sally: princess

Salochini: with beautiful eyes

Salomi: peace

Salonee: beautiful dark girl

Saloni: beautiful

Salwā: solace

Samā: of a peaceful nature, equanimity, similarity, a year

Samadu: daughter

Samajyā: fame, reputation

Samākhyā: fame, celebrity, name

Samālee: collection of flowers

Samangini: complete in all parts

Samantha: listener, blend of Sam and Anthea

Samardhukā: prospering, succeeding, daughter

Samasti: reaching, attaining, totality, universe

Samatā: equality, fairness, benevolence, peaceful

Sambhavi: another name of Durga, a kind of blue flowering sacred grass

Sambhuti: birth, origin, manifestation of night

Sambuddhi: perfect knowledge, perception

Samedi: moving one

Sameechi: praise, eulogy

Sameehā: desire, wish

Sameerā: entertaining companion

Samhitā: sacred book

Sami: exalted, saint

Samira: pleasant

Samishā: dart, javelin

Samiti: committee, herd, senate

134

Samati: harmony, agreeable, desire, wish, homage, knowledge, love, order, request

Sammā: sky

Sampad: perfection, attainment, accomplishment, blessing, fate, glory, success

Sampada: goddess Laxmi, money, wealth

Sampāngi: with a balanced body, a flower

Sampatti: prosperity, accomplishment, being, concord, welfare

Sampreeti: complete satisfaction, joy, delight

Sampriyā: dear, beloved

Sampūjā: reverence, respect

Sampushṭi: perfect prosperity

Samrāj: ruling over all

Samrāṭ: universal queen

Samriddhi: prosperity, excellence, fortune, perfection, wealth

Samridhi: prosperity

Samridhin: accomplished, perfect, blessed, happy, full of riches, Ganga

Samriti: meeting, coming together

Samudramahishi: chief wife of the ocean, Ganga

Samudranemi: surrounded by the ocean, earth

Samudrashree: beauty of the ocean, mermaid

Sāmudri: born of the ocean

Samyapradā: bestowing fortune

Samyogitā: union with God

Samyuktha: united

Sana: brilliant

Sanah: radiant, resplendent, bright

Sanam: idol, beloved, mistress, image

Sānandā: full of pleasure, pleasant, joyful, Lakshmi

Sanātani: eternal, ancient, permanent, Durga, Lakshmi, Saraswati

Sancharani: conveying, delivering a message, bringing near

Sandra: defender of men

Sandhya: evening

Sandhyā: twilight, meditation, union, holding together

Sāndhyakusumā: flower of the twilight, hibiscus

Sandhyārāgā: colour of twilight, red colour of the evening sky

Sandhyāvali: period of twilight

Sandra: God's helper, helper of mankind, short form of Alexandra

Sangani: companion

Sangeetā: music, symphony, chorus, concert

Sangeetha: music

Sangeeti: concert, symphony

Sangir: assent, promise

Sanheetā: collection of hymns

Sānikā: flute

Saniti: acquisition, procurement

Sanitrā: gift, offering

Saniya: moment or beyond comparision

Sānjali: with hands, hollowed and joined in prayer

Sanjana: consciousness, creator, creative

Sanjanā: one who joins, creator

Sanjiti: total victory

Sanjnā: well known, knowledge, perfect, agreement, clear understanding, consciousness, harmony, gesture, sign, token

Sanjogitā: attached, conjoined, related

Sankalpā: vow, with determination, resolution

Sankaṭā: remover of danger

Sankhyā: welfare, comfort, felicity, happiness, health

Sanmati: noble-minded

Sannam: farmer, kindness

Sannati: humility, bending down with humility

Sannidhi: divine presence, in the presence of God, God's residence

Sanoja: eternal

Sanoli: having self-penance, introspective

Sanrakta: red-coloured, beautiful, charming

Sanshati: doubting

Sansidhi: perfection, total accomplishement, success

Santani: continuing, making an uninterrupted line, harmony, music

Santanika: stretching, cream, foam, cobweb, sword blade

Santaniki: made of kalpa tree flower

Santati: continuity, offspring, progeny, race

Santhosha: joy

Santina: a saint

Santosha: content, satisfied, pleased

Santoshi: contented, satisfied

Santushti: total satisfaction, contentment

Sanumati: mountain

Sanvi: knowledge

Sanvitti: knowledge, harmony, intellect, understanding

Sanvritti: fulfilment, being, becoming, existing, happening

Sanjukta: relating to, conjoined, united

Sanya: meditative perception of the mind, three valleys

Saoirse: freedom

Saparya: worship, adoration, homage

Sapna: dream

Sapphire: beautiful, name of a jewel, name of a colour

Saptajit: conquering the elements, earth, water, fire, air, ether, mind, ego

Sara: solid, best, firm, excellent, hard, precious, valuable

Saragha: having colour, passionate, impassioned, precious, valuable

Saragha: beech tree

Sarah: princess, goddess

Saraigtu: fast-moving, air, wind

Sarala: straight, correct, honest, right, simple

Sarama: fleet-footed

Saranga: lute, fiddle

Sarangi: spotted doe, a musical inistrument

Sarani: path, road

Saranya: protector, shelter-provider, Durga

Saranyu: nimble, fleet-footed, quick

Sarasakshi: lotus-eyed

Saraswani: sweet-voiced

Saraswati: area full of pools, full of essences, river goddess, goddess of learning and music

Sarayu: name of a river

Sargini: made of parts

Sarianna: Gracious princess

Saridvara: best of rivers, Ganga

Sarika: mynah bird, confidante, Durga

Sarina: Sara, princess, goddess

Sarit: river, stream, Durga

Sarita: moving, river, stream

Saroja: lotus

Sarojini: abounding in lotuses

Sarupa: uniform, beautiful, handsome, embodied, similar

Sarva: complete, perfect, whole

Sarvamangala: universally, auspicious, Durga, Lakshmi

Sarvani: omnipresent, perfect, Durga

Sarvapa: drinking everything

Sarvasaha: all-enduring, earth

Sarvasanga: going with all

Sarvāstrā: with all weapons

Sarvayashā: famous among all

Sarveshā: goddess of all

Sarveshi: desired by all

Sarvikā: universal, all, entire, whole

Sasa: help, aid

Sasha: defender of mankind

Sashrikā: having beauty, grace, fortune, lovely, splendid

Sashṭhi: praise, hymn, Durga

Sasikala: art of moon, moonlight, digit of moon

Saskia: protector of the universe

Satara: princess

Sati: truthful, virtuous, faithful, Durga

Sāti: gift, offering, obtaining, gaining

Satidevi: Parvati

Satpreetikā: beloved of truth

Sattvikā: of true essence, energetic, pure, spirited, true, vigorous, Durga

Satvanti: full of truth, faithful

Sātvati: pleasant, delighted

Satvati: truthful, faithful

Satvika: truth, peaceful

Saumyā: moon-related, calm, pearl, gentle, Durga

Savannah: grassland, treeless plain

Savitā: sun

Savitri: name of a daring lady who fought with Yama (God of death) and brought back life to her husband

Sāvitri: daughter of Daksha

Savni: goddess Lakshmi

Seana: feminine form of Sean (John)

Seema: border, limit

Seeta: name of Shri Rama's wife

Selena: goddess of the moon

Selene: moon

Selika: loved by many

Selimā: peace

Selma: God's protection

Selvi: wealth

Semanti: white rose

Semantikā: white rose

Senjitā: vanquishing armies

Serap: mirage

Serafina: name of a saint

Serena: serene, calm

Serenity: serene, calm

Sesharatnam: crown jewel

Sevā: worship, devotion, homage, reverence

Sevati: white rose

Shabarā: spotted, variegated

Shabari: variegated

Shabnum: dew, snow

Shābhramati: full of water, cloudy

Shabnam: dew

Shacchandrikā: wonderful moonlight

Shachi: might, aid, farmer, grace, dexterity, kindness, skill

Shachikā: graceful, kind, skilled, dextrous

Shadiya: singer

Shaely: fairy

Shagufā: bud, blossom

Shahla: queen

Shahnaz: king's glory

Shaila: river

Shailajā: daughter of the mountain, Parvati

Shailakanyā: daughter of the mountain, Parvati

Shailasā: dweller of mountains, Parvati

Shailendrajā: daughter of the mountains, Ganga

Shaili: carved in rock, custom, habit, style, visage

Shaina: beautiful

Shaivālini: river

Shaivi: prosperity, auspiciousness

Shakambari: herb-nourishing, Durga

Shakeela: beautiful

Shakini: goddess of herbs, helpful, powerful, Parvati

Shakira: grateful

Shakti: Parvati

Shaktimati: powerful

Shaktiyashas: with a lot of fame

Shakuni: auspicious object, lucky omen

Shakunika: a bird

Shakuntala: daughter of Viswamitra and Menaka, mother of King Bharat and wife of King Dushyant

Shakuntika: small bird

Shakyra: thankful

Shala: river

Shalabha: grasshopper, locust

Shalada: procurer of spear

Shalaka: spark

Shalavati: owning a house, housewife, lady of the house

Shalibeth: daughter of peace

Shalika: parrot

Shalina: courteous, fennel

Shalini: with a fixed abode, established, domestic, modest, shy, settled

Shalisa: name of a place

Shallaway: beautiful Jasper

Shalmalini: red silk-cotton tree

Shalyn: stars over water

Shama: calm, peaceful, tranquil, lamp

Shamani: tranquillity, peace

Shamani: calming one, night

Shambavi: goddess of health, wealth and courage

Shambhari: blue-flowering sacred grass, Durga

Shambhavi: Parvati

Shambhu: helpful, kind, generous

Shambhupriyā: dear to Shiva, Durga

Shammehā: peaceful

Shāmilee: containing fire, garland

Shamili: dark

Shamirā: chameli flower

Shampā: lightning

Shana: wise, old, God is gracious

Shancy: elegant lady

Shāṇḍili: collector

Shandra: chandra, moon, Church of the fortress

Shandy: name derived from Shan or cham meaning English wine

Shane: an alternate form of Shana

Shani: marvel, wonder, an African name

Shania: on my way

Shani Hadia: marvellous gift

Shankarā: causer of tranquillity

Shankari: wife of Shankar (Shiva)

Shankhā: flute

Shankhadhaval: as white as a conchshell, jasmine

Shankhalikā: flawless, as perfect as a conchshell

Shankhamuktā: conchshell and pearl conjoined, mother of pearl

Shankariñi: having branches, supreme among branches, best, excellent

Shankhyauthikā: collection of conchshells, garland of jasmine

Shankini: mother of pearls

Shanna: beautiful

Shannara: goddess, princess

Shannon: wise

Shanshā: praise, blessing, charm, invocation, wish, recitation

Shansitā: desired, longed for, wished, celebrated

Shāntā: calm, peaceful

Shānti: tranquillity, peace

Shāntidevi: goddess of peace

Shantivā: bearer of peace, friendly, kind, beneficent

Shārada: lute bearer, veena bearer, Durga

Shāradamañi: jewel among lutes, the best lute

Sharadashree: beauty of autumn

Sharadayāmini: night in autumn

Shāradi: autumn, day of full moon, modest, sky

Sharadi: as lovely as autumn

Shāradikā: autumnal

Shāradvati: with a lute, autumnal

Sharalyn: flat plain

Shari: Sarah, princess, goddess

Sharieli: princess of God

Sharik: God's child, one on whom the sun shines

Shārman: a fair share

Sharmila: modest, happy

Sharojyotsnā: autumnal moonshine

Sharani: protecting, defending, housing, earth

Sharāvati: full of reeds

Sharde: honour confers a crown

Sharee: bird, arrow

Sharleen: little and womanly

Sharmaine: a form of Charmaine

Sharmi: industrious

Sharmilā: shy

Sharmishṭha: most fortunate

Sharon: a princess, exotic princess

Sharvā: Shiva's wife, Parvati

Sharvāñi: night

Shashankvati: like the moon

Shashi: hare-marked, an apsara, moon

Shashibhās: moonbeam

Shashikala: part of the moon, like the moon

Shashikanta: beloved of the moon, while lotus

Shashilekha: a part of the moon

Shashimukhi: moon-faced

Shashini: containing the moon, a part of the moon

Shashiprabha: moonlight

Shashirashmi: moonlight

Shashthi: praise, hymn, Durga

Shasta: tribal name, name of a mountain

Shasti: praise, hymn

Shatadala: with a 100 petals, white rose

Shatadruti: flowing in branches

Shatakara: knower of 100 skills

Shatakshi: 100-eyed, night, Durga, dill

Shatapadma: lotus with 100 petals, consisting of 100 lotuses, beautiful, loving, soft, tender

Shataparva: with 100 parts

Shataprabha: radiant, brilliant, lustrous

Shatapushkara: consisting of 100 blue lotuses

Shatapushpa: consisting of 100 flowers, extremely beautiful, with a fragrant body

Shatarupa: with a 100 forms

Shatodara: slender-waisted

Shatrunjaya: conquering enemies

Shatvari: night

Shauna: god is gracious

Shaveena: god is gracious

Shawna: slow waters

Shay: courteous, gift

Shayla: palace, fairy

Shaylin: fairy palace

Shayma: sleeping goddess, Durga, Yamuna

Shayna: pretty woman, beautiful

Shazia: priceless

Shea: courteous, gift

Sheba: name of a kingdom in southern Arabia noted for its great wealth

Sheechi: flame, glow

Sheela: calm, tranquil, good-natured

Sheelavati: virtuous, ethical

Sheena: God is gracious

Sheephalika: coral jasmine tree

Sheetal: cool, pleasant feeling

Sheetala: cold, cool, calm, gentle, passionate, moon

Sheetalata: cooling power

Sheetamanjari: blossom of the cold, coral jasmine tree

Sheetashi: cold eater

Sheetika: coldness

Sheetoshna: cold and hot

Sheila: virtue, gentle

Shela: musical

Shelby: ledge estate, willow farm

Shelly: meadow on the ledge

Shemushi: intellect, wisdom, understanding

Sheneeza: God is gracious

Shephali: like drowsy bees, very fragrant, coral jasmine tree

Shephalika: a fruit of mycanthes (coral tree)

Sheri: cherished one

Sheridan: bright

Sheryne: an amazing, beautiful girl

Sherry: short form of Sharon

Sheva: prosperity, happiness, homage

Shevalini: with a mass-like surface

Shey: courteous, gift

Shibani: Parvati

Shikha: crest, flame, peak, pinnacle, ray of light, topknot

Shikhandi: crested, yellow, jasmine

Shikhandini: peahen

Shikharvasini: dwelling on a peak, Durga

Shikarini: eminent, excellent, Arabian jasmine

Shikrā: skilful, able, artisitic, clever

Shilā: rock

Shilavati: virtuous, moral

Shiloh: the one to whom it belongs

Shilpa: sculpture

Shilpā: variegated

Shilpi: artisan

Shilpikā: skilled in art

Shilyā: mountains

Shimidā: giving work

Shingā: tinkle, jingle, tinkling of silver ornaments

Shiphā: whiplash, tuff of hair on crown of head

Shiprā: cheeks, rose

Shiralee: the swagmans swag, the burden

Shirdena: female variant of Sheridan

Shireesha: a delicate flower

Shiriña: night

Shirley: country meadow

Shishugandha: with a youthful fragrance, double jasmine

Shital: calm, quiet, cool, pleasant feeling

Shivā: auspicious power, goddess of grace, final liberation, Parvati, Durga

Shivadevi: goddess of grace-prosperity-welfare

Shivadūti: Shiva's messenger, Durga

Shivadūtikā: Shiva's messenger

Shivakāntā: beloved of Shiva, Durga

Shivakāriñi: doer of kind deeds, goddess of welfare, Durga

Shivakarñi: producer of prosperity

Shivāli: beloved of Shiva, Parvati

Shivāni: Parvati

Shivapriyā: beloved of Shiva, Durga

Shivasundari: wife of Shiva, Parvati

Shivātmikā: soul of Shiva, consisting of Shiva's essence

Shivikā: palanquin

Shobā: pretty, lovely, beautiful

Shobanā: beautiful, turmeric

Shobha: shining, glow

Shobhana: shining, glowing, one who glows, the bright one

Shobhikā: brilliant, beautiful

Shobhini: graceful, wonderful

Shobhishtha: most beautiful, splendid

Shochayanti: inflaming

Shochi: flame

Shoki: night

Shoṅā: redness, fiery

Shorṅamaṇi: red gem, ruby

Shoṅita: red, saffron flower

Shraddhā: faith, loyalty, confidence, trust, reverence

Shradha: Lakshmi goddess

Shravishṭhā: most famous

Shree: diffusing radiance, conjoining of beauty-grace-prosperity, grace, glory, light, majesty, power, splendour, Indian lotus

Shreya: to give credit to someone

Shreyā: best, beautiful, excellent

Shrilātā: divine maiden

Shribhadrā: best among people

Shridā: given by Lakshmi, bestowing fortune

Shridevā: giver of fortune

Shridevi: goddess of prosperity, Lakshmi

Shrihara: excelling in all beauty

Shrihastini: in the hands of fortune, sunflower

Shrikā: born of Shree, prosperity, fortune, wealth, beauty

Shrikala: a part of Lakshmi

Shrikamya: desirous of glory

Shrikanthika: graceful-voiced

Shrila: given by Lakshmi, beautiful, eminent, happy, prosperous

Shrilalita: graceful, prosperous

Shrilata: divine vine

Shrimangala: goddess of prosperity

Shrimani: best among jewels, beautiful jewel

Shrimati: bearer of prosperity, beauty, divine, graceful, pleasant, royal, Spanish jasmine

Shrimukhi: with a radiant face

Shrina: night

Shrinandini: daughter of prosperity

Shrishti: mother nature

Shrivani: divine speech

Shrividya: divine knowledge, Durga

Shria: goddess Lakshmi

Shriya: prosperity and happiness

Shringarika: love

Shringini: crested, cow, jasmine

Shrinjayi: giving victory

Shrujal: dedicated

Shruta: famous, celebrated, glorious, heard, known

Shrutadevi: goddess of knowledge, Saraswati

Shrutakeerti: of well-known glory, famous

Shrutasoma: of the moon

Shrutashravas: listener of the scriptures

Shrutavati: favourably known

Shrutavinda: knower of the scriptures

Shruti: hearing, ear, knowledge of the *Vedas*

Shrutibuddhi: with knowledge of scriptures

Shubha: splendour, beauty, desire, decoration, light, lustre, ornament, assembly of gods

148

Shubhada: auspicious

Shubhaga: going well, gracious, elegant

Shubhalochana: fair-eyed

Shubhamala: with a splendid garland

Shubhamayi: full of splendour, beautiful, splendid

Shubhananda: delighting in virtues

Shubhangi: with beautiful limbs

Shubhankari: doer of good deeds, virtuous, Parvati

Shubhasuchani: indicating good

Shaubhavaktra: of auspicious face

Shubhika: garland of auspicious flowers

Shubhra: radiant, Ganga

Shubhravati: fair-complexioned

Shubhru: lovely browed woman

Shuchi: sacred, pure

Shuchimallika: white vine, Arabian jasmine

Shuchimukhi: pure-face

Shuchinta: deep thought

Shuchismati: shining, radiant

Shuchismita: with a pious smile

Shuddha: clearness, purity, holiness, truth, Durga

Shukavani: parrot-voiced

Shuki: parrot, bright, quick-witted, talkative

Shukla: white, pure, bright, Saraswati

Shukti: beautiful verse, wise saying

Shuktimati: having oyster shells

Shubadhara: bearing a spear, Shiva's wife, Durga

Shuladharini: holding a spear, Durga

Shulini: armed with a spear, Durga

Shūraputrā: with a heroic son

Shveni: white

Shwetā: white

Shwetāmbarā: clad in white

Shweti: whiteness

Shwitrā: white

Shyla: daughter of the mountain, goddess Parvati

Shyāmā: dark, beautiful, blue, black

Shyamālā: dark, Durga

Shyanne: an American tribal name

Shyeti: white

Shylāh: loyal to God, strong

Sian: god is merciful

Sibani: Parvathi

Sibyl: prophetess, oracle

Siddhalakshmi: perfect, fortune, Lakshmi

Siddhambā: blessed mother, Durga

Siddhānganā: an accomplished woman

Siddharthā: attainer of meaning, attainer of wealth

Siddhavati: achieving perfection

Siddhayogini: perfect yogini (fairy, magician)

Siddhi: accomplishment, acquisition of magical powers, fulfilment, luck, prosperity, success, Durga

Siddhidātri: bestower of perfection, Durga

Siddirūpini: goddess of achieving all

Siddhyāyikā: accomplisher, fulfiller, effector

Sidhumātri: mother of streams, Saraswati

Sidney: name of a city, from St.Denis

Sidonia: from Sidon

Sienna: name of a city, brownish red colour

Sierra: mountains, mountainous

Sierrah: adventurous spirit

Sigrid: beautiful, victorious.

Siham: arrows

Sijenna: god is gracious

Sila: ancient river

Silvana: woodland, forest

Silvia: wood, forest

Simbala: a small pod, flower of Shalmali tree

Simon: hear, listen

Simone: hear, listen

Simran: remember

Sin: beneath the legends

Sindhu: ocean, sea, river

Sindhujā: ocean-born, Lakshmi

Sindhukanyā: daugher of the ocean, Lakshmi

Sinead: variant of Jane

Sinhamati: lion-hearted, courageous

Sinhi: lioness

Sinhikā: lioness

Sinhini: lioness

Sinkhumar: porpoise

Siri: wealth, beautiful, victorious

Sirinā: night

Sirisha: sacred, delicate flower

Sitā: white, sugar, moonlight, pretty woman

Sitara: name of a musical instrument

Sitārā: star

Sitasindhu: pure river, Ganga

Sitayāmini: moonlight

Skylana: heaven's light

Skylar: scholar

Sloane: fighter, warrior

Smaradhwajā: bright moonlit night

Smaradūti: messenger of love

Smarani: act of remembering

Smerā: smiling, blossomed, apparent, evident, friendly

Smita: smiling

Smitha: smile

Smriti: remembrance, desire, code of laws, understanding, wish

Smritimala: garland of memories

Smruthi: guideline, rememberence

Sneha: affection, friendliness, love, tenderness

Snehal: full of affection

Snehalata: vine of love

Sneha Latha: friendly girl

Snehamayi: loving

Sneya: life of the oceans

Snigdha: innocence

Snigdha: friendly, attached, agreeable, charming, glossy, intent, resplendent, shining, tender

Sofia: variant of Sophia (wisdom)

Sohana: graceful, beautiful

Sohani: beautiful

Sohela: beautiful

Sohini: adorned, beautiful, splendid

Solana: sunshine, eastern wind

Solange: solemn, dignified, name of a saint, angel of the Sun

Soma: the moon

Soma: soma plant, moonlike, beautiful

Somabha: like the moon

Somada: like a moon, bestower of tranquillity, producer of nectar

Somadevi: goddess of nectar

Somadhara: Milky Way, stream of soma

Somalata: creeper from which soma is extracted

Somali: beloved of the moon

Somashree: divine nectar

Somasuta: daughter of the moon

Somavati: containing soma

Sona: gold

Sona: gold

Sonakshi: golden-eyed, Parvati

Sonal: gold

Sonāli: golden, Indian laburnum

Sonālikā: golden

Soni: golden, beautiful

Sonia: wise, wisdom

Soniā: Parvati

Sonikā: with golden beauty

Sonilā: moonlike, calm

Sonu: gold, beautiful

Sony: gold

Sonyā: wisdom

Sophia: wisdom, wise

Sophie: familiar form of Sophia

Sorah: sea shell

Soraya: princess, constellation

Soujanya: courtesy

Soumya: patient girl

Soundarya: beauty

Sovā: one's own

Spandanā: heart-throb, pulsating beauty

Sparshānand: delighting the touch

Spurthi: drive, encouragement, stimulation

Spring: season

Sraavya: sweet to listen either in speech or singing

Sraddha: faith, trust, confidence, reverence, loyalty, interest, concentration

Sragvini: wearing a wealth of flowers

Sravanthi: stream, a river, continuous flow

Sravanti: flowing

Sreelatha: divine vine

Sreshta: the best, the great

Sri Devi: Lakshmi

Sri Gowri: Parvati

Srija: Lakshmi

Srikalā: art of God

Srilahari: wave

Srilakshmi: Lakshmi

Srilasya: Sri stands for goddess Lakshmi and lasya implies the graceful aspect of dance

Srinjayi: giving victory

Srishti: universe, world

Sriti: path, road

Srivalli: wife of snake god

Srividya: Saraswati

Srujana: good creativity

Srushty: whole earth

Sruthakeerthi: fair and glory

Sruti: veda

Stacey: resurrection

Stacia: resurrection

Starla: star, astonomical name meaning star

Star Skye: a nickname

Stāvā: praiser

Stāvarā: stable, steady, still, firm, constant, immovable

Stella: star

Stephanie: the crowned one, crown, wreath

Sthirā: strong-minded, earth

Streeratnā: jewel of a woman

Streetmā: complete woman

Stuthi: praise God, hymn

Stuti: praise, adulation, eulogy

Subakee: very strong, very powerful

Subāndhav: good friend

Subani: good vani (voice)

Subhā: auspicious, glorious, splendid, Durga

Subhada: giver of prosperity

Subhāgā: fortunate, rich

Subhāryā: prosperous lady, graceful lady

Subhāshani: soft-spoken

Subhashini: good speaker

Subhashitā: spoken well of

Subitā: comfort

Subudhi: of good intellect, clever, understanding, wise

Suchārā: very skilful, good performer

Suchara: with a beautiful gait

Suchhāyā: casting a beautiful shadow, beautiful, shining, brightly, splendid

Suchitā: sacred, propitious

Suchitrā: well marked, having auspicious marks, distinguished, manifold, variegated

Sudāmā: generous

Sudāmini: as bright as lightning, wealthy, light

Sudanti: with good teeth

Sudarshanā: lovely in appearance, pleasing to eyes

Sudarshini: pretty, comely, lotus pond

Sudattā: well-given

Sudeeksha: girl with strong determination

Sudeeptha: light with good hope

Sudeshnā: born in a good place

Sudevi: real goddess

Sudhā: welfare, comfort, honey, ease, good drink, nectar, soma, water, lightning, Ganga

Sudhakshina: very sincere

Sudānshuratna: jewel of the moon

Sudehsna: name of Virata Queen

Sudeshnā: King Virat's wife

Sudha: nectar, amrit

Sudhamayi: sweet girl

Sudhanvita: one who is full of nectar, pleasant, charming

Sudharmā: right path, follower of laws

Sudhi: intelligence, good sense

Sudheksha: beautiful, consecration, Lakshmi

Suditi: bright flame

Sudrishi: pretty, eye-pleasing, with beautiful eyes

Sugaña: good attendant

Sugandhā: fragrant, basil

Sugandhi: fragrant, blue lotus, small banana

Sugandhikā: fragrant

155

Sugati: bliss, happiness, welfare

Sugatri: graceful, fair-limbed

Sugeshna: singing well

Sugreevi: with a beautiful neck

Suguna: one with good habits

Suhasini: smiling beautifully

Suhela: easily accessible

Suhita: beneficial, suitable

Suja: good birth

Sujaashri: a great wealth

Sujala: cloud

Sujasa: of good fame

Sujata: well-born, noble, pretty

Sujaya: a great triumph

Sujjvala: clear

Suka: rejoicing

Sukala: good part, very skilled

Sukanthi: sweet-voiced

Sukanya: beautiful maiden

Sukeshi: with beautiful hair

Sukla: pleasure, comfort, ease, piety, virtue

Sukhada: giver of happiness, Ganga

Sukhavati: happy

Sukeerti: well praised, hymn of praise

Sukeshini: with beautiful hair

Sukhita: pleasure

Sukreeda: sporting

Sukrita: pious deed, doing good

Sukriti: auspiciousness, good conduct, kindness, virtue

Sukshi: beautiful verse, wise saying

Sukamari: very tender, very delicate, soft

Sukusuma: adorned with pretty flowers

Sulabha: easily available, jasmine

Sulakshana: with auspicious marks, fortunate, with good qualities

Sulakshmi: divine Lakshmi, divine wealth

Sulakshini: beautiful woman

Sulekha: good writer

Sulekhā: having auspicious line, fortunate

Sulochana: one with beautiful hair

Sulochanā: with beautiful eyes

Sulochitā: very red

Sulomā: with beautiful hair

Suma: flower

Sumadātmajā: daughter of passion

Sumadhyā: graceful woman, slender-waisted

Sumaiah: name of a companion of Prophet Muhammad and mother of Ammar-i-Yasir, who is considered the first woman martyr of Islam

Sumaiya: high

Sumālini: well garlanded

Sumāllikā: geese, beautiful shuttle

Suman: a person with good soul, flower

Sumana: one who have good heart or mind

Sumanā: beautiful, charming, lovely, wheat, Spanish jasmine

Sumangatā: auspicious

Sumangali: auspicious, Parvati

Sumantikā: Indian white rose

Sumati: good mind, devotion, generosity, kindness

Sumārali: garland of flowers

Sumāyā: with excellent plans

Sumayyah: name of a companion of Prophet Muhammad and mother of Ammar-i-Yasir, who is considered the first woman martyr of Islam

Sumedha: having a brilliant mind, intelligent

Sumehrā: beautiful face

Sumiko: child of goodness, beautiful child

157

Sumīrā: much remembered, overtly praised

Sumitā: with a balanced form, with a beautiful body, well measured

Sumitrā: nice friend, having many friends

Summer: a nature name, name of a season used as girl's name

Sumnāvarī: bringing joy

Sumonā: quiet, calm

Sumrini: rosary

Sumukhi: bright faced, learned, lovely, pleasing

Sumuṇḍika: with a good head, sensible

Sunaina: one with beautiful eyes

Sunakshatrā: born under an auspicious constellation

Sunāmi: well-named

Sunandā: pleasing, delighting, Parvati

Sunandi: pleasing, delighting

Sunayā: very first, well conducted

Sunayanā: with beautiful eyes

Sundaravati: having beauty

Sundari: beautiful

Suneetā: of blue colour, very dark

Suneelimā: bright blue, dark

Suneeti: good conduct, wisdom, discretion

Sunehrị: golden

Suneta: one with good morals

Suniksha: one with beautiful ornaments

Sunitā: well conducted, civil, polite, well behaved

Sunithā: moral, righteous, virtuous, well disposed

Sunnidhi: divine presence, in the presence of God, God's residence

Sunshāntā: perfectly calm

Sunny: sunshine

Suntana: beautiful girl

Sūnvitā: joy, exultation, gladness, kindness

Suparña: with beautiful leaves, Parvati

Suphulla: with beautiful blossoms

Suprabha: very bright, beautiful, splendid

Suprabhat: illuminated by dawn, morning prayer

Supraja: with many children

Suprasada: auspicious, gracious, propitious

Suprateekini: with beautiful form

Supratishtha: well established, consecration, famous, glorious, installation

Suprayoga: well managed, well practised, dextrous

Suprema: very loving

Supriti: great joy, great delight

Supriya: very dear, lovely

Supunya: bearer of good deeds, of great religious merit

Supushpa: with beautiful flowers

Sura: wine, spirituous liquor

Surabhi: sweet-smelling, agreeable, beautiful, beloved, charming, famous, pleasing, wise, shining, virtuous, basil, jasmine, earth

Surabhu: born of the gods

Suradevi: goddess of wine

Suraja: born of the Gods

Surajani: beautiful night

Surakamini: desired by the Gods

Surala: bringer of Gods, Ganga

Suranya: very beautiful

Surana: gay, joyous, making a pleasing sound

Surananda: joy of the Gods

Surangana: celestial woman

Surapriya: dear to the Gods

Surasa: of good essence, elegant, lovely, sweet, well flavoured, basil, Durga

Surastri: celestial woman

Surasū: mother of Gods

Surasundari: celestial beauty, Durga

Surathā: with a good chariot

Suratnā: possessing rich jewels

Suravāhini: river of the Gods, Ganga

Suravalli: vine of the Gods, basil

Suravāni: earth

Suravarā: best among the Gods

Suravilāsini: heavenly nymph, apsara

Surbalā: female deity

Sureeli: in time

Sureetā: melodious

Surejyā: worshipped by the Gods, sacred basil

Surekha: godess Lakshmi

Surekhā: having beautiful lines, auspicious, fortunate

Surenū: very small, dust particle, an atom

Sureshi: supreme goddess, Durga

Sūri: wife of the sun

Suri: goddess

Surmyā: good-looking

Surochanā: much liked, beautiful, enlightening

Surohi ni: beautifully red

Surtā: divine truth

Suruchā: bright light, with fine tastes

Suruchi: taking pleasure in

Surukhi: with a pretty face

Surūpā: well formed, beautiful, lovely, Spanish jasmine

Surūpika: well formed, beautiful

Sūryā: wife of Sun God

Suryabhā: as bright as the Sun

Sūryajā: born of the sun

Sūryakalā: a part of the sun

Sūryakānti: sunshine, sunlight

Sūryalochanā: eye of the sun, with bright eyes

Sūryamukhi: sun-faced, bright face, sunflower

Sūryāni: wife of the sun

Sūryaprabhā: as bright as the sun

Sūryashobhā: sunshine, as beautiful as the sun

Suryashree: divine sun

Susan: lily

Susangatā: good companion, easily attainable

Susannah: a form of Susan

Suseela: one with good conduct

Sushila: one with good conduct

Sushmā: exquisite beauty, splendour

Susatyā: always truthful

Sushila: well disposed, good tempered

Sushilika: of good character, a bird

Sushmita: one with a pleasant smile

Sushobhanā: very charming, very graceful

Sushravā: very famous, well known

Sushree: very rich, extremely splendid

Sushubhā: very auspicious, very beautiful

Sushyāmā: very beautiful, very dark

Susimā: with the hair well parted

Susmitā: with a pleasant smile

Suswarā: sweet-voiced

Sutā: begotten, daughter

Sutanu: slender, delicate

Sutārā: very bright, twinkling star, cat's eye

Sutārakā: with beautiful water, sparking water

Sutrāmā: protecting well, earth

Surachā: speaking well

Surachani: always speaking well, lute

Suvali: graceful

Suvāmā: beautiful woman

Surachalā: abode of a glorious life

Suvarchas: full of life, very glorious

Suvarṇā: golden-linked, gold, turmeric

Suvar ñarekhā: golden line

Suvārtā: good news, bringer of good tidings

Suvāsini: fragrance

Suvāsu: fragrant

Suvedā: very intelligent, very knowledgeable, know of scriptures

Suveṇā: with beautifully plaited hair

Suvithi: good knowledge, divine being

Suvratā: very religious, virtuous wife

Suvitā: well behaved, good, virtuous

Suvyūhā: halo

Suyashā: very famous

Suyashas: very famous

Suzanne: lily

Suzu: long lived, spring, autumn child

Svea: unique

Svetlana: a very bright star

Swadhā: self-power

Swadhi: well minded, thoughtful

Swakriti: good looking

Swamini: lady of the house

Swapnā: dream

Swapnasundari: dream girl

Swapnil: dreamy

Swarā: goddess of music, goddess of musical notes

Swaradevi: knower of music, goddess of music

Swarbhānavi: daughter of the divine, daughter of the sun

Swareñu: beautiful note

Swargangā: Milky Way, celestial Ganga

Swarna: gold

Swarñā: golden

162

Swarnalatā: golden wine

Swarnamālā: golden necklace

Swarñāmbhā: white light, golden light

Swarñapadmā: having golden lotuses, celestial Ganga

Swarnapushpikā: golden flower, jasmine

Swarnarekhā: golden streak

Swaroop: good looking

Swārshā: celestial, bestowing light

Swarūpā: beautiful

Swarneethi: heavenly path, abode of music

Swaryoshit: celestial woman

Swasti: well being, success, fortune

Swasū: self-created, earth

Swathya: goddess Durga

Swāti: one of the seven onstellations, the star Arcturus

Swayamprabhā: self-shining

Swetha: white, fair complexion

Swikriti: acceptance

Sybil: prophetess, oracle

Sydney: name of a city

Sylaja: Parvati

Sylvia: forest

Sylvie: a maiden of the forest

Syona: lucky

T

Tabitā: gazelle

Tabitha: deer

Tacey: peace, silence

Taconnis: a bold, intelligent, and out-going person

Tadiprabhā: flash of lightning

Taevy: angel

Tahela: sing praises unto God

Tahirāh: chaste, pure

Tahlia: darkness

Takara: precious

Talākākshi: with green eyes

Talākhyā: perfume

Talia: joyous, muse of comedy, blooming

Talikā: palm of the hand, nightingale

Talli: young, boat, youthful

Talsim: miracle, wonder, enchantment

Taluni: maiden

Tamā: night

Tamahārinī: dispeller of darkness

Tamarin: palm tree

Tamarind: exotic spice

Tamasā: dark-coloured

Tāmasi: night, sleep, Durga

Tamasvini: night

Tami: night

Tāmrā: copper-crested

Tāmrajākshi: copper-eyed

Tamrakarnī: ears of copper hue

Tāmrapakshā: copper-hued

Tāmraparnī: with red leaves

Tāmrarasā: of red juice

Tāmravati: coppery

Tāmrikā: coppery

Tanatswa: purified

Tanaya: daughter

Tanecia: beautiful African princess

Tanis: a form of Tanya

Tanu: beautiful, excellent

Tanūbhavā: daughter

Tanūjā: born of the body, daughter

Tanulatā: with a vine-like body, supple, slender

Tanushree: with a divine body

Tanveer: delicate woman

Tanuvi: slender woman

Tanvangi: slender-limbed

Tanvi: slender, delicate, beautiful, fine

Tanya: fairy queen, angel, dark, empowerer

Tanyā: daughter

Tapanasutā: daugher of the sun, Yamuna

Tapanatanyā: daughter of the sun

Tapanātmajā: daughter of the sun, Yamuna

Tāpani: heat

Tapanti: warming

Tapasvini: devoted to God

Tapaswini: ascetic

Tapati: warming

Tāpi: heat, glow

Tārā: star, pupil of the eye, perfume, meteor, rocky

Tārābhūshā: adorned with stars, night

Tārādattā: given by the stars

Tarah: high hill

Tāraka: falling star, meteor, star, eye

Tarakeswari: Parvati

Tārakini: starry night

Taralā: spirituous liquor, bee

Tārāmati: with a glorious mind

Tārāmbā: mother star

Tārānā: song

Tarangini: full of waves, moving, restless

Tarani: boat, raft

Tārāpushpa: star blossom, jasmine

Tārāvali: multitude of stars

Tārāvati: surrounded by stars, Durga

Tārikā: belonging to the stars

Tarin: blend of Tara and Erin

Tāriṇi: enabling to cross over, saving, Durga

Tārinnerā: crossing over the water, possessing liberating quality

Tarishi: a raft, a boat, the ocean, daughter of Indra

Taritā: forefinger, leader, Durga

Tarnijā: Yamuna

Tarpiṇi: satisfying, hibiscus, offering oblations

Tarryn: blend of Tara and Erin

Tarulatā: vine

Taruṇi: young girl

Tarushi: victory

Tasli: comfort, peace

Tatalā: repetitive, Durga

Tatikshā: endurance, patience

Tātripi: intensely satisfiying

Tatum: surprised, different

Tātum: cheerful, joy-bringer

Tavishi: power, courage, heavenly virgin, strength, river, earth

Ṭawnie: little one, yellowish-brown

Taya: perfectly formed

Taylor: tailor, surname

Tejamayi: Lalithamba's other name

Tejasri: Lalithamba's other name, with divine power and grace

Tejaswari: Lalithamba's other name

Teerthā: passage, ford, place of pilgrimage, way, sacred object, water

Teerthamayi: having pilgrimage centres

Teerthanemi:

circumbulating, carrying sacred objects, the sacred place,

Teerthavali: pious, holy, flowing through a sacred place

Tejashree: with divine power, divine grace

Tejasvati: energetic, bright, glorious, splendid

Tejasvita: nobility, radiance

Tejini: sharp, energetic, bright, whetstone, touchstone

Tejomayi: consisting of light, full of splendour

Tejovati: bright, sharp, splendid

Teju: Lalithamba

Tejwanti: radiant

Terence: variant of Roman clan name

Tessa: short form of Teresa

Tessia: short form of Teresa

Tessie: short form of Teresa

Thakuri: deity

Thalia: joyful or blossoming

Thana: gratitude

Thara: wealth

Theophilos: friend of God

Thistle: plant with thorns

Thoyajakshi: born in water. Lakshmi

Thushara: name of a flower

Tiara: crowned

Tiannah: princess

Tiffany: goddess, God's appearance, manifestation of God

Tilabhavani: beautiful dot, jasmine

Tilaka: type of necklace

Tilakalata: ornamental vine

Tilakavati: decorated

Tilika: marked with sandal paste

Tilla: preceder

Tilotama: damsel of great beauty

Timi: fish

Timila: a musical instrument

Tina: illustrious, a river

Tintisha: a tree

Tipti: daughter of Sun god

Tiree: beautiful trees

Tishyarakshita: protected by luck

Titiksha: endurance, patience

Titli: butterfly

Titus: a Greek Christian missionary to whom Paul wrote the canoncial letter Titus.

Tomi: rich

Tonya: priceless, beyond price, invaluable

Tori: bird

Toshani: pleasing, satisfying, appeasing, gratifying, Durga

Toshi: mirror reflection

Toshita: satisfied

Toya: water

Toyaneevi: girdled by ocean, earth

Trayee: intellect, understanding

Treesha: desire

Treya: treading the three paths

Triambika: wife of three-eyed Shiva, Parvati

Tridhara: stream with three tributaries, Ganga

Tridiva: heaven, cardamom

Trigarta: woman, pearl

Trihayani: returning in three years

Trijagati: mother of the three worlds, Parvati

Trijama: night

Trijata: with three locks of hair

Trikala: of three pieces

Trilochana: wife of the three-eyed Shiva, Parvati

Trinaina: Durga

Tripta: contentment, satisfaction, Ganga

Tripti: satisfaction

Tripura: triply fortified, Durga

Triputā: threefold, Arabian jasmine, Durga

Trishalā: three-pointed

Trishlā: thirsting, deserving

Trishnā: desire

Trishulini: wife of the trishul bearer, Durga

Trivali: blue lotus

Trive ñi: triple-braided

Triyā: young woman

Trudy: beloved

Trusha: victory

Truti: atom, a small part of time

Tudi: satisfying

Tuhi: cuckoo's cry

Tulasāri ñi: quiver

Tulasi: matchless, sacred basil

Tulika: brush

Tūlini: cotton tree

Tully: peaceful

Tungā: strong, high, elevated

Tungabhadrā: very noble, sacred

Tungaveñā: loving heights

Tungi: night, turmeric

Turavati: wind

Turi: painter's brush

Turuyā: superior powers

Tushā: longing, desire

Tushina: satisfaction

Tushitā: pleased, satisfied

Tushti: satisfaction, contentment

Tuvikshtara: ruling strongly

Twaritā: swift, quick, expenditious, Durga

Tweshā: brilliant, glittering, vehement, impetuous

Twinkle: glitter

Twishā: light, splendour

Twishi: vehemence, brilliance, energy, light, splendour, impetuosity

Tyra: untamed

U

Ucchadevatā: superior God, time personified

Ucchatā: superiority, height

Udalākāshyap : watering the earth, goddess of agriculture

Udankanyā: daugher of the ocean, Lakshmi

Udantikā: satisfaction, contentment

Udāramati: noble-minded

Udayanti: risen, excellent, virtuous

Udayati: daughter of the mountain

Udbhūti: emerging, appearance, existing, fortune-giver

Uddeepti: excited, inflamed

Udgeetā: sung, celebrated, extolled, hymn of the glory, ultimate song

Udgeeti: singing

Uditi: rising of the sun

Udu: water, star

Udvahā: carrying on, continuing, daughter

Udvahni: sparkling, gleaming

Udyati: raised, elevated

Ugrachāriṇi: moving impetuously, Durga

Ugraduhitri: daughter of a powerful man

Ugrajit: victor of passion

Ujālā: shining, radiant, luminous

Ujāli: night

Ujjayati: winner, conqueror, victory

Ujjeshā: victorious

Ujjiti: victory

Ujjivati: brought to life, full of life, jubilant, optimist

Ujjeevayati: animated

Ujjwalā: splendour, clearness, brightness

Ujjwalitā: shining, lighted, flaming

Ujwala: bright, brilliant, lustrous

170

Utharkā: praise of the sun, hymn of the sun

Uktasampadā: wealth of hymns

Ukthin: uttering verses, praising

Ukti: proclamation, idiom, expression, word, sentence, speech

Ulā: seaweed

Ulfāh: friendship, harmony, love

Ulimā: astute, wise

Ulkā: meteor, fire, torch, firebrand, falling from heaven

Ulkushi: meteor, firebrand

Uloopi: name of one of the Arjuna's wives

Ulūki: female owl

Ulūpi: with a charming face

Umā: splendour, fame, light, night, quiet, reputation, tranquillity, Parvati, Durga

Uma Devi: tranquility, Parvati

Umang: happiness

Umaymā: young mother

Umlochā: with questioning eyes

Unā: one

Unaysā: friendly, affable

Undadhisutā: daugher of the ocean, Lakshmi

Uneṭte: crowned lamb

Unice: victory

Unnā: woman

Unmadā: with intoxicating beauty, passionate

Unmādini: bewitching, intoxicating

Unmukti: deliverance

Unnati: dignity, prosperity, progress, rising

Upabhuti: enjoyment

Upaḍā: gift, offering, benevolent

Upadhriti: ray of light

Upakārikā: protector

Upakoshā: like a treasure

Upamā: resemblance, equality, similarity

Upañayikā: fit for an offering

Upaneeti: initiation

Upāsanā: devotion, homage, worship

Upashamtā: tranquillity, patience

Upashruti: listening attentively

Upāsti: worship, adoration

Upaveñā: with small tributaries

Uraniā: heavenly

Uranitā: precious metal

Uriānā: gracious light

Urilyn: beautiful light

Urishṭa: tree

Urity: purity

Ūrjā: energy, vigour, strength, breath, food, heartborn, power, water

Ūrjani: belonging to energy

Urjaswati: vigorous, powerful, juicy

Urjjasvati: full of energy, strong

Ūrmi: ripple, wave, light

Ūrmikā: wave, hum of bees, finger ring

Ūrmila: of the waves of passion, beautiful, enchanting

Ūrmyā: wavy, night

Ūrña: woollen, warm, ever excited

Urooj: height, exaltation

Ursula: little she bear

Ursullā: female bear

Urukeerti: of far-reaching fame

Urunjirā: pleaser of heart, hear-winning

Urushā: granting much, producing plentiful

Urutā: greatness, vastness

Uruvi: great, broad, excellent, large, spacious, earth

Urvanā: fairy

Uravarā: fertile soil, earth

Urvashi: widely, extending, Ganga

Urvi: wide one, earth

Urvija: Sita

Usha: daybreak, dawn, morning light

Ushama: summer

Ushas: dawn, morning light

Ushalakshi: dawn-eyed, large-eyed, with piercing, eyes

Ushi: wish

Ushira: fragrant root of a sacred plant

Ushma: heat, spring, passion, anger, ardour, the hot season

Ushna: with desire

Ushana: desire, wish, plant of some juice

Ushasi: twilight

Ushija: desire-born, available, charming, deserving, desirable, wishing, zealous

Ushika: worshipper of dawn

Usra: morning light, brightness, earth

Usri: dawn, morning light, daybreak

Utala: agile, quick

Uti: help, enjoyment, kindness, protection

Utina: anointed

Uthalika: yearning for glory, bud, wave

Uthalita: unbounded, blossoming, brilliant, opened, loosened

Utkanika: desire, yearning

Utkanti: excessive, splendour

Utkarika: of precious material

Utkarshini: attributes

Utkarthini: fulfilling one's ambitions

Utkashana: giving orders, commanding

Utkhala: perfume

Utkrashita: excellence, superiority

Utpala: lotus

Utshiptika: lifted, crescent-shaped earring for upper ear

173

Utkūjā: cooing note of bird

Utpala: filled with lotuses

Utpalākshi: lotus-eyed, Lakshmi

Utpalamālā: garland of lotus flowers

Utpalāvati: made of lotuses

Utpalini: collection of lotuses

Uttamā: best, affectionate, excellent

Uttami: best woman

Uttamikā: best worker

Urgā: strong, Kali

Urveejā: born of the earth

Utpala: lotus, water lily

Usr: day break

Uru: big

Uttara: name of a star, daughter of king Virata and wife of Abhimanyu

Uttarā: higher, upper, northern, future, result

Uttarikā: crossing over, emerging, conveying, delivering, boat

Uttejini: exciting, animating

Utūki: female falcon

Uvā: breath of life

Uzimā: great

Uzmā: the greatest

Uzuri: beauty

Usrā: day break

Urutā: vastness

Upada: offering

Urvijya: victory of the earth

V

Vāchā: speech, oath, voice, word, sacred text

Vāchaknavi: with the power of speech, speaker, orator, eloquent

Vadhusarā: mobile woman

Vāgdevi: goddess of speech, Saraswati

Vageeshwari: goddess of speech, Saraswati

Vahini: flow

Vāhini: body of force, army

Vahnijāyā: conqueror of fire

Vahnikanyā: daughter of fire, air, wind

Vahnipriyā: beloved of fire

Vahnishwari: goddess of fire, Lakshmi

Vahyakā: chariot

Vaidagdhi: grace, beauty

Vaidehi: princess of the Videhas, Sita

Vaidhriti: with a similar disposition, properly adjusted

Vaijayanti: gift of victory, flag, garland of victory, banner

Vaijayantikā: bestowing victory, banner, flag, pearl necklace

Vaijayantimālā: garland of victory

Vaikunthā: without hindrance, abode of the absolute

Vaimitrā: friend of the universe

Vairāgi: free from passions

Vaishali: name of an ancient city

Vaishāli: the great

Vaishālini: daughter of the great

Vaishnavi: worshipper of Vishnu

Vaitarañi: helper in crossing over to the other world

Vaivasvati: belonging to the sun, Yamuna

Vajrā: mighty, strong, hard, Durga

Vajradehi: diamond-bodied

Vajrajivālā: shining like lightning

Vajramālā: with a diamond necklace

Vajrashree: divine diamond

Vajravalli: useful vine, sunflower

Vāka: word, speech, recitation, text

Vākapradā: giver of speech, Saraswati

Vākini: reciter

Vakshanā: nourisher, bed of a river, refreshing

Vakshani: strengthening

Vakshi: strength, nourishment, flame

Vakti: speech

Vala: chosen

Valashiphā: curled hair

Valli: wife of Karthikeya

Valyā: coiled, armlet, bracelet, ring

Vālguki: very beautiful

Vālini: with a tail, constellation Ashwini

Vallabhā: beloved

Vallaki: lute

Vallari: cluster of blossoms, creeper, Sita

Vallarikā: vine

Vallāri: vine

Valhi: creeper, vine, lightning, earth

Vallikā: covered with vines, covered with greenery

Vāmā: beautiful, Durga, Lakshmi, Saraswati

Vāmākshi: fair-eyed

Vāmālochanā: four-eyed

Vāmini: bringing wealth, short

Vāmanikā: small

Vāmikā: situated on the left side

Vanachandrikā: moon rays, of the forest, jasmine

Vanajā: forest-born, water-born, sylvan, blue lotus

Vanajākshī: blue lotus-eyed

Vanajāyatā: resembling a lotus

Vanajyotsni: light of the jungle, jasmine

Vanalatā: creeper of the forest, vine

Vanalikā: of the forest, sunflower

Vanamala: a garland made out of various flowers

Vanamālā: garland of the forest, garland of flower, flower braid

Vanamālikā: garland of the forest, garland of wild flowers

Vanamāleeshā: desired by the forest gardener

Vanamalli: wild, jasmine

Vanamallikā: jasmine

Vanāmbikā: mother of the forest

Vanapushpā: flower of the forest, wild flower

Vanarashmi: light of the forest, ray of light

Vanasorojini: lotus of the forest, wild cotton plant, collection of wild lotuses

Vanashobhanā: water, beautifying, lotus

Vanathi: of the forest

Vānchā: desire, wish

Vandanā: adoration, praise, worship, prayer

Vandanikā: praised, honoured

Vanditā: praised, worshipped

Vandyā: praiseworthy, adorable

Vanessa: a beautiful butterfly

Vāni: desire, wish

Vānichi: speech

Vānimayi: goddess of speech, Saraswati

Vānini: soft-voiced, intriguing woman

Vanisha: pure

Vanishka: flute

Vānishree: divine speech, Saraswati

Vanisree: Saraswati

Vanita: desired, wished for, loved, woman

Vanjula: a cow full of milk

Vankshu: arm

Vanmayi: goddess of speech, Saraswati

Vansa: goddess

Vansha: offspring, daughter, lineage, bamboo

Vanshadhara: carrying on the race

Vanshalakshmi: family fortune

Vanshi: flute, pipe, artery

Vanshika: flute

Vanu: eager, zealous, friend

Vanya: treasure, wealth, chosen, valuable

Vapra: garden bed

Vapu: body

Vapusha: embodied, beauty, very beautiful, handsome, nature

Vapushi: embodied, wonderfully beautiful

Vapushmati: having a form, beautiful

Vapushtama: best among the embodied, wonderfully beautiful

Vara: boon, benefit, blessing, choice, gift, reward, Parvati

Varada: giver of boons, girl, maiden

Varajakshi: with lotus eyes

Varalika: goddess of power, Durga

Varana: encompassing, surrounding, enclosing, rampant

Varanana: with a beautiful face

Varanari: best woman

Vara nashi: granting boons

Varangana: beautiful

Varangi: with a beautiful body

Varangi: with a graceful form, turmeric

Varapakshma: well feathered

Varaprada: granting wishes

Vararoha: elegant, fine, handsome, fine rider

Varastree: noble woman

Varasyā: desire, request, wish

Varavamini: with a beautiful complexion, Durga, Lakshmi, Saraswati

Vardhini: developing, improving, strengthening

Vāree: rich in presents, goddess of speech, water, Saraswati

Varee: stream, river

Vareñyā: desirable, Shiva's wife, saffron

Varga: belonging to a set or group

Varijaksha: lotus-eyed

Varisha: monsoon

Varivasyā: devotion, honour, obedience, service

Varja: water-born, lotus

Varñapushpi: coloured flower, amaranth lily

Varñika: of fine colour, fine gold, purity of gold

Varoyashit: beautiful woman

Varsha: rain, monsoon

Vārshika: belonging to the monsoon, yearly, jasmine

Vārta: news, tidings, intelligence

Varunā: goddess of water

Varuñāni: water-born, Lakshmi

Varuni: godess of intoxication

Vāruṇi: of water, resembling water, wine, liquor

Varūthini: multitude, army, troop

Varūtri: protector

Vāsana: knowledge from past experience, desire, fancy, imagination, inclination, motion

Vasantaja: born in spring, jasmine

Vasantakusum: spring flower

Vasantalatā: vine of spring

Vasantalekhā: spring-written, spring-born

Vasantasenā: with spring as army commander, as charming as spring

Vasantashree: beauty of spring

Vāsanti: of the spring season, light yellow, saffron

Vasantikā: goddess of spring

Vasāti: dawn

Vasavadattā: enticing, fragrance-born, given by Indra

Vāsavi: daughter of the all-pervading

Vasāvi: treasury

Vashā: obedient, willing

Vashitā: bewitching

Vashti: beautiful one

Vasitā: woman

Vasordhārā: stream of wealth, celestial Ganga

Vastri: shining, illumining

Vastu: dawn, morning

Vasu: light, radiance

Vasudā: granting wealth, earth

Vasudāmā: controlling the divine beings

Vasudattā: given by the Gods

Vasudevā: goddess of wealth

Vasudhā: producing wealth, earth, Lakshmi

Vasudharā: bearing wealth

Vasudhāriñi: bearer of treasures, earth

Vasudhiti: having wealth

Vasulakshmi: divine goddess of wealth

Vasumati: having treasure, earth

Vasundhara: the earth

Vasundharā: abode of weath, containing wealth

Vasundhareshā: wife of the lord of the earth

Vasundhareyi: daughter of the earth, Sita

Vasuprabhā: divine light

Vāsurā: valuable, night, earth, woman

Vasushree: divine grace

Vasvi: divine night

Vasvoksārā: essence of divine waters

Vātansā: garland, ring, crest

V ātarūpā: with the form of wind, subtle, transparent

Vatieka: unique and strong

Vātikā: Ved Vyas's wife

Vatshā: child-loving, affectionate, devoted, loving

Vatsamitrā: friend of children, friend of calves

Vatū: speaker of truth

Vayā: branch, twig, child, power, strength, vigour

Vayodhā: invigorating, strengthening, refreshing

Vayuñā: moving, alive, active, mark, aim, goals, wisdom, knowledge

Vayuvegā: swift as the wind

Vedā: well-known, famous, meritorious, pious

Vedabhā: obtained from knowledge

Vedajanani: mother of the *Vedas*, Gayatri mantra

Vedamātri: mother of the *Vedas*, Saraswati, Gayatri

Vedanā: knowledge, perception, pain, discomfort

Vedāsini: carrying wealth

Vedashree: beauty of *Vedas*

Vedashruti: heard about in the *Vedas*, famous in *Vedas*

Vedavati: knower of the *Vedas*

Vedeshvā: born of the sacred texts

Vedhasyā: worship, piety

Vedi: knowledge, altar, science

Vedikā: making known, seal ring, restoring to consciousness

Vedini: knowing, feeling, announcing

Vedna: knowledge, perception

Vedyā: knowledge

Veekshā: knowledge, intelligence

Veena: a musical instrument

Veeña: lightning, lute

Veendu: dot, point, intelligence, wisdom

Veerā: brave, excellent, heroic, powerful, strong, wise

Veerabālā: brave maiden

Veerāni: brave woman

Veerendri: goddess of the brave

Veerikā: possessed with bravery

Veeriñi: of whom the brave are born, mother of some

Veerudhā: sprouting, formed, grown

Veeryā: vigour, energy, strength

Veeryavati: powerful

Veeti: enjoyment, fire, light, lustre

Vegā: falling star

Vegavahini: flowing fast

Vegavati: rapid

Vemā: goddess

Veñikā: constantly flowing

Vennela: moonlight

Vera: faithful

Verity: truth

Veronica: true image

Verity: truthful

Vesna: slavic godess of springtime

Vesta: keeper of the house

Vianca: princess, goddess

Vibha: bright, radiant

Vibhāsanā: glitter, shine

Victoria: victory

Vidipitā: lighted

Vidhuvati: beautiful woman

Vidnā: fate, destiny

Vidyā: spiritual knowledge, learning

Vidyādevi: goddess of learning

Vidyādhari: learning knowledge

Vidyāgauri: goddess of knowledge

Vidyullatha: lighting plant

Vidyāvadhū: presiding goddess over learning

Vidyāvati: learned

Vidyotā: consisting of lightning, glittering, shining

Vidyudvalli: flash of lightning

Vidyudvar ña: lightning coloured

Vidyudyotā: with the brightness of learning

Vidyulatā: creeper of lightning

Vidyullekhā: streak of lightning

Vidyutā: lightning, dawn, flashing thunderbolt

Vidyutparña: having lightning as wings

Vidyutprabhā: flashing like lightning

Vihā: heaven

Vihangi: a bird, one that flies

Vikasatikā: gentle laughter, smiling

Vijarā: ever young

Vijayā: victorious, triumphant, Durga

Vijayata: winner

Vijayeta: winner, conqueror

Vijayshantikā: finally victorious

Vijayshree: glory of victory

Vijayvati: victorious

Vijiti: victory, triumph

Vijittāri: vanquisher

Vikachashree: with radiant beauty

Vikāshini: shining, radiant, illuminant

Vikhyāti: fame, celebrity

Vikrānti: all-pervading, heroism, might, prowess, strength

Vikunṭhā: inward glance, penetration, mental concentration

Vilāsmayi: playful, graceful, charming

Vilāsanti: flashing, glittering, shining

Vilāsini: radiant, charming, lively, playful, shining, Lakshmi

Vilochanā: beautiful eyes

Vilohitā: deep red

Vimalā: flawless, stainless, clear, pure, sacred, spotless, bright

Vimalamati: pure in heart

Vimi: goddess

Vimochani: freedom, emancipation, liberation

Vinamratā: gentleness, modesty, politeness

Vinatā: humble, a bower

Vinati: prayer, humility, entreaty, modesty

Vinay: politeness

Vināyvati: polite, modest, gentle

Vindā: auspicious time

Vindu: water drop

Vineela: deep blue

Vineeta: humble

Vineeti: modesty, good conduct, training

Vinila: deep blue

Vinoda: joy, happiness, fun

Vinodini: humorous, witty

Vinoditā: amused, delighted, diverted

Vipā: speech

Vipachitti: sagacious

Vipanchi: remover of troubles

Vipāshā: unbound, chainless

Vipodhā: inspiring

Vipsā: repetition, succession

Vipulā: great, abundant, large, earth

Vipulekshaṇā: large-eyed

Virajā: clean, dust-free, pure

Virajini: brilliant, splendid, queen

Virendri: goddess of the brave

Virochanā: shining upon, illuminating

184

Virūpā: manifold, variegated, altered

Visala: large, spacious, extenstive, wide

Vishālā: large, extensive, spacious, wide

Vishalākshi: large-eye, Durga

Vishalyā: relieved from pain

Vishirā: with no prominent veins

Vishnu: omnipresent

Vishnumati: with omnipresent intelligence

Vishnumāyā: illusion of Vishnu, Durga

Vishnupriyā: beloved of Vishnu, wax flower, Lakshmi

Vishobhaginā: prosperous, Saraswati

Vishokā: exempted from grief

Vishruti: fame, celebrity

Vishtāreni: large, might, extensive, expansive, spreading

Vishuddhi: purity, sacredness, virtue, perfect knowledge, holiness

Vishwā: earth

Vishwadhārini: abode of the universe, all-maintaining, earth

Vishwadhenu: cow of the universe, all-feeding, earth

Vishwagandhā: fragrance of the universe, fragrance, all-pervading, earth

Vishwamalā: enchanting the universe, all-delighting, all-consuming

Vishwambhari: feeding the universe, all-bearing, earth

Vishwamukhi: of the universe

Vishwapāvani: pious in the universe, sacred basil

Vishwapūjitā: worshipped by all, sacred basil

Vishwaruchi: illuminator of the universe, all-glittering

Vishwarūpā: with the form of the universe, multicoloured, many-coloured

Vishwarūpikā: with the form of the universe

Vishwarūpi ṇi: with the form of the universe, creator of universe

Vishwasahā: all-enduring

Vishwavati: possessing the universe, universal, Ganga

Vishweshā: lady of the universe, desired by all

Vitanā: extension, abundance, heap, oblation, performance, plenty

Vitolā: very calm

Vittadā: giver of wealth

Vitti: acquisition, gain, finding

Vivandishā: wish to worship

Vivasvati: shining forth, diffusing light

Vivian: full of life

Vivianne: gracious, vibrant

Viviette: vibrant, full of life

Vivitsā: desire for knowledge

Vivyan: vibrant, full of life

Viyadgangā: celestial ganga, galaxy

Voletā: veiled one

Vonessā: butterfly

Vreni: verity, truth

Vrichayā: searching

Vriddhā: great, eldest, experienced, large, learned, wise

Vriddhakanyā: daughter of preceptor

Vrindā: swarm, flock, cluster of flowers, all, many, choruses of singers, heap, sacred basil

Vrishakā: cow

Vrittamallikā: encircling creeper, jasmine

Vritti: existence, being, moral conduct, state

Vūrnā: chosen, selected

Vyāpti: accomplishement, attainment, omnipresence

Viyashṭi: attainment, individuality, singleness, success

Vumā: mother

Vyatibhā: shining forth

Vyeni: variously hued, dawn

Vyāgree: tigress

Vyāghrritee: speech

Vyāpti: accomplishment

Vyomagangā: celestial Ganga

Vyomini: celestial

Vyshalani: natural beauty

Vyushṭi: first gleam of dawn, beauty, felicity, grace, fruit, reward, prosperity

Vyoma: the sky

Vyomika: reside in the sky

Vyominee: heavenly

W

Waheedā: exquisite, beautiful

Waiyā: beautiful pearl

Wamikā: a goddess

Wamilā: beautiful

Wanā: turtle dove

Wanda: wanderer, traveler

Wava: stranger

Wendy: friend

Wendy: fair

Weslee: feminine form of Wesley

Wesley: from the west meadow, feminine form of Weslee

Weslia: feminine form of Wesley

Whitely: white meadow

Whitney: pure white, fair island

Widjan: ecstacy

Willa: resolute protector

Willo: a willow tree noted for its slender, graceful branches and leaves

Winifred: reconciled, blessed

Winnie: reconciled, blessed

Winona: first born daughter

Winter: the season

Wulandari: full moon

Wynne: light-complexioned

X

Xandra: variant of Alexandra

Xandria: variant of Alexandra

Xanthe: yellow blonde

Xanthia: yellow blonde

Xavia: bright, splendid

Xaviera: bright, splendid

Xela: goddess of love

Xena: hospitable, welcoming

Xenia: welcoming, hospitable

Xuxa: nickname of Susana

Xyla: woodland

Xylia: woodland

Xylina: woodland

Y

Yādavi: woman of the Yadava tribe, Durga

Yadunandini: daughter of the Yadus

Yadvā: perception, intelligence, mind

Yagaseni: daughter of fire

Yahvā: heaven and earth, flowing water

Yahvat: everflowing waters

Yajā: worshipper, sacrificer

Yajaira: worshipper

Yajnikā: offering to God

Yakshāngi: alive, speedy

Yakshi: female protector of forests, quick, speedy, supernatural being

Yakshini: another name for Yakshi

Yamakālindi: blossoming

Yamalā: twin

Yamamā: a valley

Yamee: elder twin sister, pair, couple, brace

Yāmee: motion, progress, path, road, carriage, course

Yāminā: right and proper

Yāmini: consisting of watches, night

Yamuna: river

Yāmyā: night

Yara: princess

Yashasvati: famous, illustrious

Yashasvini: beautiful, famous, illustrious, splendid

Yashodā: conferring fame, Durga

Yashodevi: goddess of fame and beauty

Yashodhā: conferring splendour and fame

Yashodharā: maintaining fame and glory

Yasholekhā: narrative of glorious deeds

Yashomati: having fame

Yashovati: possessing fame and glory

Yashtika: string of pearls

Yashvita: famous and successful

Yashwarya: fame & prosperity

Yasmeen: jasmine flower

Yasmin: jasmine

Yasmina: jasmine flower

Yasmine: jasmine flower

Yati: restraint, control, guidance

Yatudhani: magician, conjurer

Yavanika: stage

Yazmin: jasmine flower

Yedda: singing

Yemaya: goddess of the ocean, mother of all

Yesenia: flower

Yessenia: variant of Llesenia

Ynes: chaste

Ynez: chaste

Yoga: total, meditation, conjunction

Yogadeepika: light of meditation

Yogamaya: magical power of abstract meditation, Durga

Yoganidra: meditation sleep

Yogaratna: magical jewel

Yogasiddha: yoga-perfected

Yogatara: chief star of a constellation

Yogavati: joined, united, versed in yoga

Yogeshwari: adept in yoga, Durga

Yogin: meditator, ascetic, devotee

Yogini: with magical power, fairy, sorceress

Yogita: enchanted, bewitched, wild

Yojana: plan

Yoko: positive child or female

Yolanda: the flower violet, the French form of violet and the Hungarian Jolanda

Yolia: feminine heart

Yonina: little dove

Yori: reliable

Yosha: young woman, maiden

Yoshana: girl, young woman

Yoshi: blessed

Yoshidratna: jewel among women

Yoshino: respectful, good

Yoshita: woman, wife

Young: eternal wealth

Yovela: rejoicing

Ysabel: medieval form of Isabel

Yubhika: numerous

Yue: moon

Yugal: pair

Yugandhara: bearing an era, earth

Yuliana: downy-haired

Yuliya: downy-haired

Yulisa: truth, noble

Yuki: blessed, snow

Yuko: gracious child

Yumna: good fortune, successful

Yumi: beautiful

Yumiko: arrow child

Yun: cloud

Yuriko: lily child

Yusra: prosperous

Yuthika: multitude, white jasmine

Yuvateeshta: yellow jasmine

Yuvika: jasmine

Yvette: fiminine form of Yves

Yvette: yew tree

Yvonna: feminine variant of Yves

Yvonne: feminine variant of Yves

Yvonnita: yew tree, gracious

Z

Zade: happy

Zafeerā: firm

Zafinā: victorious

Zafirā: successful, victorious

Zāharā: shining, luminous

Zaheeraa: expression

Zāhidā: abstinent

Zāhirā: obvious

Zahrā: white, flowers

Zaidā: fortunate

Zaina: xenia

Zairā: visitor, rose

Zākirā: one who remembers Allah regularly

Zakiya: pure

Zakulā: intelligent

Zalika: well born

Zameelā: companion

Zamrud: narrator of the Hadith

Zandra: Alexandra

Zaneta: name of a saint

Zanie: lily, form of Susan

Zaqirā: witty

Zara: princess

Zareen: golden

Zareenā: companion of Prophet Mohammad

Zarina: golden

Zarinaa: queen

Zarqā: blue

Zaynā: great

Zaynāb: Prophet Mohammed's daughter

Zaytoon: olive

Zebidiah: magical

Zeenat: glory

Zelda: short form of Grizelda

Zelma: Selma

Zenia: name of a flower, welcoming

Zenobia: name of a queen

Zenouska: little maid

Zenzele: she will do it herself

Zereen: golden

Zetana: name derived from Zeta, sixteenth letter of Greek Alphabet

Zeynep: name of Prophet Mohammad's child

Zhane: Jenae

Zia: splendour, light

Zita: name of a saint

Zivah: radiant

Zoe: life

Zoey: life

Zohra: blossom

Zohraa: jupiter

Zora: dawn

Zoya: life, a form of Zoe

Zsa Zsa: pet name for Susan

Zuleika: fair-haired

Zulekhaa: beautiful

Zulemā: peace

Top 50 Girls Names in England and Wales

1. Chloe
2. Emily
3. Megan
4. Jessica
5. Sophie
6. Lauren
7. Charlotte
8. Hannah
9. Olivia
10. Lucy
11. Ellie
12. Amy
13. Katie
14. Georgia
15. Rebecca
16. Molly
17. Bethany
18. Emma
19. Holly
20. Ella
21. Caitlin
22. Abigail
23. Grace
24. Jade
25. Mia
26. Shannon
27. Eleanor
28. Alice
29. Jasmine
30. Courtney
31. Leah
32. Amelia
33. Elizabeth
34. Anna
35. Amber
36. Lily
37. Laura
38. Sarah
39. Rachel
40. Phoebe
41. Erin (New Entry)
42. Millie (New Entry)
43. Zoe
44. Abbie
45. Nicole
46. Paige
47. Niamh
48. Daisy
49. Natasha
50. Alexandra

Top 50 Girls Names in Scotland

1. Chloe
2. Amy
3. Lauren
4. Emma
5. Megan
6. Erin
7. Hannah
8. Rebecca
9. Sophie
10. Caitlin
11. Rachel
12. Emily
13. Katie
14. Lucy
15. Nicole
16. Shannon
17. Ellie
18. Sarah
19. Morgan
20. Abbie
21. Niamh
22. Anna
23. Eilidh
24. Olivia
25. Holly
26. Zoe
27. Laura
28. Courtney
29. Cara
30. Eve
31. Molly
32. Jade
33. Kirsty
34. Leah
35. Aimee
36. Jessica
37. Beth
38. Charlotte
39. Taylor
40. Jennifer
41. Jodie
42. Heather
43. Abby
44. Samantha
45. Robyn
46. Lousie
47. Rachael
48. Bethany
49. Georgia
50. Iona
51. Kayleigh

More titles are available in

GENERAL BOOKS

1.	Brain Ticklers in English	80/-
2.	Brain Ticklers in General Knowlege	110/-
3.	Brain Ticklers in Nature	80/-
4.	Business Letter	90/-
5.	A Book of Stenography	95/-
6.	Baby Names for Girls	75/-
7.	Baby Names for Boys	75/-
8.	Science Quiz	95/-
9.	World Quiz	95/-
10.	Facing Job Interviews	125/-
11.	How to Reduce Tension	125/-
12.	How to Succeed in Life	125/-
13.	How to be Fit & Young	95/-
14.	Grow Rich with Peace of Mind	125/-
15.	Helpline for Stressed Parents	125/-

4263, Street No. 3, Ansari Road,
Daryaganj, New Delhi-110002
Ph.: 32903912, 23290047, 9811594448
E-mail: lotus_press@sify.com
Website: www.lotuspress.co.in